RESPONSIBLE USE OF THE INTERNET IN EDUCATION

Issues Concerning Evaluation, Citation, Copyright, and Fair Use of Web Materials

by

Professor Aniekan Ebiefung

D1255567

PENMAN PUBLISHING, INC.

RESPONSIBLE USE OF THE INTERNET IN EDUCATION

Issues Concerning Evaluation, Citation, Copyright, and Fair Use of Web Materials

by

Professor Aniekan Ebiefung

University of Chattanooga Foundation Professor
The University of Tennessee at Chattanooga, TN USA

ISBN 0-9720775-3-7

Dedication

To my family: Anne, Ediobong,
Uduak, and Mary Anne

And

To all teachers who are not afraid
to try new technologies

Acknowledgement

I would like to thank the 40 teachers from the Hamilton County School System who attended the Tennessee Higher Education Commission funded workshop on Teaching Mathematics Using the Internet. Their honest discussions and responses to questions during the workshop contributed immensely to the development of this project.

My thanks also go to my friends and colleagues who read the manuscripts and offered invaluable suggestions. In particular, I am indebted to Jim Bowman, Deborah Arfken, and Wade Rittenburger.

My special thanks to Ray and Mary Lee Hammond, of Penman Publishing, for their honest and unalloyed suggestions for the book and about publishing in general.

Finally, I acknowledge the love, understanding, and support of my wife and children during some of the sleepless nights.

A.A.E.

Preface

The Internet is a set of computers linked together by communications lines. It has been successfully used in commerce and in personal communication. Many educators are experimenting on how to best use this communication medium to advance the processes of teaching, research, and collaborative projects.

This book examines the set of issues involved in using the Internet for education in a responsible and effective way. As with other technologies used in education, the effect the Internet will have in the learning process will depend on how it is actually utilized in the classroom. To assist in the proper use of the Internet in the classroom for teaching, research, or in Internet communication projects, this book discusses in Part I the advantages and disadvantages of using the Internet in education, the factors that will lead to a successful use of the Internet in teaching, and suggests those educational activities that seem more natural for use on the Internet.

Carrying out research using the Internet requires the use of search tools to locate different sources of information. However, it is difficult to navigate the Internet without wasting a great deal of time in the process. To derive any substantial benefit in using the Internet for research, one must learn to search effectively for information on his or her research topic. When the needed information is finally found, it must be preserved and used in a responsible manner. This book discusses how to do so in Part II.

Anyone with access to a Web server can post materials on the Internet. Consequently, any information obtained from the Internet must be evaluated for accuracy and for meeting educational needs. On the other hand, using the Internet for collaborative projects involves e-mails, chat rooms, video conferencing, and bulletin boards to communicate with persons in different places all over the world. The challenge, however, is to determine the best projects that suit ones needs among the thousands of communication projects available on the Internet, and getting involved in these projects in a responsible way. This book discusses how to evaluate Web materials and collaborative projects in Part III.

Many ethical issues must be considered when using Internet materials or communicating using Internet communication channels. In Parts IV and V this book discusses citation of Internet materials, online netiquette, copyright and fair use, and acceptable use policies.

The purpose of this book, therefore, is to assist readers in developing a balanced view about the implications of using the Internet for education. It is my belief that such knowledge is essential for an effective and responsible use of the Internet in Education, especially under conditions of limited resources that many nations are facing today.

The Internet is a dynamic medium. It continues to evolve at a very rapid rate. This means that some of the web sites listed in this book may change over time. If this happens, do not worry. Use a search engine to find the resources you need.

May you enjoy the exciting world of the Internet in your educational activities!

Usage

This book will be valuable to anyone who uses the Internet for teaching or who helps children use the Internet for research or collaborative projects. The book can also be used as a supplement to courses in Educational Technology offered in colleges of education, which relate to teaching using the Internet. It may also be used as a supplement to general education courses in computer literacy where students are expected to master the rudiments of effective use of the Internet.

This book contains information from teaching instructional guides on how to use the Internet in the classroom. Thus the book naturally satisfies the in-service needs of many K-12 teachers and school administrators. College professors will find this book to be an important source of references on effective and responsible use of the Internet.

Dr. Aniekan Ebiefung, Professor of Mathematics
University of Tennessee at Chattanooga
August 2002

Table of Contents

Part I

Why Use the Internet for Education

Educators want to replicate the success stories of Internet use in commerce and in personal communication in education. They believe that properly used, the Internet has a potential to enhance the learning process. To assist the educator use the Internet effectively in education, the book explains in Chapter 1, how the brain assimilates new information and how the Internet can assist in the assimilation process. As with other technologies used in education, the effect the Internet will have in the learning process will depend on how it is actually utilized in the classroom. To assist in the proper use of the Internet in the classroom, this book discusses in Chapter 2 factors that will lead to a successful use of the Internet in teaching as well as the advantages and disadvantages of using the Internet in education. In Chapter 3, we point out that not all-educational activities can be successfully done on the Internet, and then discuss those educational activities that seem more natural for use on the Internet.

Chapter 1

The Internet and the Learning Process

1.1 How we Assimilate New Information

One of the main reasons we teach is to assist the student in acquiring knowledge, information or skills that will help the student become a useful member of the society. This observation begs the following questions? How do we assimilate information? How could the Internet enhance the assimilation process?

The answer to the first question can be represented by the oversimplified illustration of the brain in Figure 1. As the diagram explains, information received in the senses first goes to the short-term memory, which does not store information for a long time. If conditions are conducive, the information goes to the long-term memory through the sphincters. Otherwise, the information is flushed out.

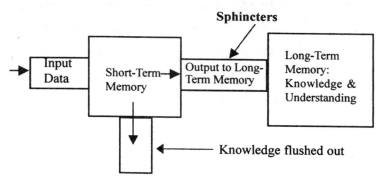

Figure 1-1: The brain's assimilation process

We now use an example to demonstrate the consequences of this assimilation process. Suppose a teacher gives an examination to a class of twenty students and ten students get B's. If she then gives the same exam again after two weeks to the ten students who got the B's, how many of them will get B's for the second time? There is no definite answer to this question. It depends on how each student was able to transfer the skills needed for the exam from the short-term memory to the long-term memory. Students who moved all the facts from the short-term memory to the long-term memory, where there is understanding, should be able to get B's or even A's on the second examination. On the other hand, students who were not able to move all the facts tested from short-term memory to long-term memory should be expected to get less than B's.

An ideal learning process, as the above example suggests, should enable all students to transfer all the information learned from short-term memory to long-term memory. As you have probably guessed, this is not an easy task. Nor is it the duty of the teacher alone. Both the student and teacher have roles to play in the transfer process.

The student's responsibility is to find the template and hooks that fasten the information to their long-term memory. To do this, the student should be able to **discover** and **own** the knowledge. How can a student do that? The following example shows it is possible, and also the best way to go about it. In my trigonometry class in high school, we learned that the values of all the trigonometry functions are positive in the first quadrant. Moreover, the values of the sine and its reciprocal, the values of the tangent and its reciprocal, and the values of the cosine and its reciprocal are positive in the second, third, and forth quadrants, respectively. Some of us came up with the mnemonic, CAST, where C means the cosine and its reciprocal are positive in the fourth quadrant, and so on, as explained in Figure 2.

S Sine and Cosecant are positive	**A** All trigonometry functions are positive
T Tangent and Cotangent are positive	**C** Cosine and Secant are positive

Figure 1-2: Mnemonic for the signs of the trigonometric functions.

Any time I say or hear the word *cast,* I remember the lesson and the facts. This is only one example of how to discover and own knowledge. There are other ways. In fact, many students in the class had different ways of remembering the same facts from the lesson. Have you in the past used a process similar to this? This is a good skill to teach your students. In the next section, we summarize how the Internet can assist the student in the assimilation process.

Your responsibility as a teacher is to facilitate, promote, and expedite the transfer of information from short-term memory to long-term memory. To accomplish this task, you must provide avenues and an environment in which your students can create, discover, and own their knowledge. The Internet can assist you to accomplish this task as described in the next section.

1.2   How the Internet Enhances the Teaching Process

You can use the Internet to manage your classroom or improve the planning and delivery of your lessons as listed below. This list is by no means exhaustive, and I hope you would come up with other creative ways of taking advantage of the Internet for your teaching.

1.   Providing Students with Motivation: You want to teach using the Internet because you want to change, improve, and add a new dimension to your teaching, or you want to vary the types and increase the quality of activities assigned to your students. This is your motivation, the driving force behind your reading books or attending seminars that relate to teaching using the Internet.

In a similar vein, your students need some motivation. Allowing your students to use the Internet in their learning is a motivational push to students who are bored by the traditional ways of information delivery, and thereby expedite the transfer of information from short-term memory to long-term memory. I believe that one of the attributes of a good teacher is the ability to motivate the "lost" student, the ability to reach out to the unreachable in his/her class. The Internet allows you to motivate some of the lost students in your classes, and thereby accelerate the assimilation process.

2. Questioning and Discovery: According to an African proverb, *A person who asks questions understands a new language faster*. Some subjects, such as mathematics, are like new languages to many of our students. You should encourage and provide your students with avenues to ask questions. Good questions by you can excite interest in a rather boring subject. Using the Internet for educational activities provides a different avenue for discovery through questioning, and for critical evaluation of information.

It is also important that you answer students' questions properly and quickly. This is why you must constantly retrain according to the needs of the time. For this information age, you must be armed with the personal and educational uses of the Internet. If not, you stand to be embarrassed by some of your students.

3. Communicating and Using Knowledge: The constant use of knowledge enhances understanding and long-term memory. Using knowledge in different settings gives you a better understanding of the different shades of meaning of the concepts involved in a given learning situation. Communication is a way of using knowledge.

It is a source for re-enforcement. The Internet promotes fast communication across geographical barriers, and therefore gives students an opportunity to communicate early in life with a broad range of people never before imagined possible.

4. **Well-designed Lesson Plans**: The resources and communication capabilities of the Internet provide an opportunity to creatively design integrated lesson plans and assignments that combine problem solving, writing, critical thinking, discovery, and exploration. Properly designed, such lessons allow and encourage students to ask questions and be involved in the learning process, and to be the creators of their own knowledge. For an example, in Teaching Mathematics with the Internet Workshop, with Web site http://www.utc.edu/~thecmath, participants were coached to develop such integrated lesson plans. In addition, there are numerous quality lesson plans on the Internet, which you can download free and modify to suit your particular classroom needs.

5. **Professional Development**: Professional development is a key to updating skills and for career advancement. You can use the Internet to join a discussion group, subscribe to a news group, take classes, and keep in touch with professional colleagues.

6. **Class Management**: You can post class lessons, homework problems, and practice exams on the Net for students to access from home, from the library, or from any place that has access to the Net. Parents can access the class Web pages to confirm the homework problems their children are required to do. It is also possible to

structure the homework in such a way that the student can progress from simpler to more challenging activities by means of hyperlinks.

In addition to posting class lessons and homework, you can have a class bulletin board on your Web site. In this way, or by a mailing list, students can get involved in class discussions in a manner not possible in the classroom. This medium can also be used to resolve problems between class periods. For example, suppose there is no class for two days before an exam. If one of the students e-mails a question to you that may be of interest to other students in the class, then before the exam you could post such a question and the answer on the bulletin board or send it to all students through the mailing list.

Thus the Internet allows you to add content to your lessons and to disseminate useful information to students and parents without wasting valuable class time.

7. Examination Administration: There is plentiful software available, such as Web Course in a Box, which allows you to give and grade exams on the Internet. This provides some degree of flexibility that could be used to accommodate students who have genuine reasons not to take the exam at a given time.

A major problem with online testing is security. To prevent cheating, the exam could be given in a laboratory setting whereby a student has to identify himself or herself before taking the exam. You may also consider making it possible for each student to take different versions of the same examination.

8.   Ease of Lesson Presentation: If you publish your lesson on the Internet, it allows you to color code or graphically present key concepts. As mentioned before, you can also use hyperlinks to direct students to related materials. Thus, you can use the Internet to enhance the quality of your classroom presentation.

Figure 1-3: Unlike the use of blackboard, the Internet enhances the
quality of your classroom presentation by
allowing you to use multiple media.

Chapter 2

How Internet Affects the Learning Process

As was pointed out in Chapter 1, the Internet, apart from boosting your role as a coach, provides some students with the tools they need to discover and own knowledge. It therefore gives these students the hooks and templates they need to fasten information to the long-term memory.

On the other hand, use of the Internet for education is not without problems. It comes with a price, which, if not properly addressed, can derail the learning process. Since the Internet is a dynamic medium, at least for now, one should expect the problems to be encountered in using the Internet in teaching to be evolving as well. The following paragraphs outline the advantages and disadvantages of using the Internet in teaching. Also discussed is the key to successful use of the Internet in Education.

2.1 Advantages

Below is a summary of some key reasons you should encourage your students to use the Internet in their learning.

1. **Motivating Factor:** The Internet can act as a motivating tool for many students. Young people are captivated with technology. Educators must capitalize on this interest, excitement, and

enthusiasm about the Internet for the purpose of enhancing learning. For already enthusiastic learners, the Internet allows you to provide them with additional learning activities not readily available in the classroom.

2. **Fast Communication**: The Internet promotes fast communications across geographical barriers. Your students can join collaborative projects that involve students from different states, countries or continents. This type of learning experience was not possible before the Internet. I consider this unique learning experience essential for each of our students, as the world is becoming one big community.

3. **Possibility for Equal Playing Field:** Libraries in poor neighborhoods or countries are obviously not as well equipped as those in more affluent neighborhoods or countries. For example, the worst equipped library in the United States may be better than the best equipped libraries in some third world countries. The Internet complements the library and provides the possibility that all persons in the world, regardless of race or social status, can have access to the same study materials. This will reduce some of the advantages students in rich schools have over students in poor schools. The assumption, of course, is that in the future all persons will have access to the Internet and will be properly educated about using the Internet in an effective and responsible manner.

4. **Interactive Activities:** There are many interactive activities on the Internet for students of all ages. What could be better than students playing games and learning at the same time? While it is true that interactive activities are available through other media, unlike other media, those from the Internet are usually free.

5. **Cooperative Learning:** The Internet facilitates cooperative learning, encourages dialogue, and creates a more engaging classroom. For example, a LISTSERV for your class will allow your students to get involved in class discussions through e-mail in a way not possible within the four walls of the classroom.

6. **Locating Research Materials:** Apart from communication, research is what takes many people to the Internet. There are many more resources on the Internet than the school library can provide. Encourage your students to take advantage of this wealth of resources for their research.

7. **Acquiring Varied Writing Skills**: If students are
    required to publish their work on the Internet, they
    have to develop hypertext skills. These skills help
    students gain experience in non-sequential
    writings. Since the Internet is open to all with
    access, students who are publishing their work on
    the Internet are forced to be mindful of their
    language and to write to non-expert audience. This
    is a skill that will be useful in life after school.

8. **The Work Environment:** Many businesses have
    Web sites and some require computer skills for
    employment. Using the Internet in the classroom
    makes it possible for students to easily adapt to
    the work environment, during school time or after
    graduation. Many employers post job listings on
    the Internet and some even seek preliminary
    information through the Internet. There are also
    Internet sites that help students in their job search.
    If your students are familiar with the Internet, they
    are likely to take advantage of these jobs
    opportunities on the Internet.

2.2 Disadvantages

Following are some of the problems you may encounter when considering the Internet as one of the educational tools for your classroom. In each case, ways in which you can minimize the incidences of these problems in your classroom are suggested.

1. **Inappropriate Site**: It is very easy for students to accidentally, and sometimes deliberately, visit inappropriate sites. There are reported cases in which a search for taxes, NASA, or the White House resulted in pornographic sites. By specifying the Web sites students should use for research, or by allowing them to use only students' friendly search tools, you can minimize your students' visits to inappropriate sites.

2. **Student Privacy**: Criminals, marketers, and other persons can easily get information from students when they are online. These could post danger to students' lives or may even lead to litigation against the school. To avoid this problem, students should be educated on the dangers of giving information to people online. Parents and teachers need to supervise students' online activities.

3. **Plagiarism**: Apart from Web sites that claim to help students write term papers, there are numerous cases of students downloading information from the Net and turning it in for grades. You can minimize this problem by requiring students to cite research sources. There is also an online service called Plagiarism.org at http://www.plagiarism.org. This service claims to prevent plagiarism by determining whether a term paper has been copied from the Internet.

4. **Age Appropriate Information**: Anyone with a Web server can put information on the Internet. The levels of some write-ups are beyond the education level of students, and are therefore subject to misinterpretation. Moreover, some of the information on the Internet is wrong, adulterated, instigating, or misleading at best. Students who cannot discriminate between these types of information may become influenced in an inappropriate manner.

5. **Preparation Time**: It takes a lot of preparation time to effectively use the Net for education. In addition to designing Internet based lesson plans, you may have to surf the Internet to download lesson plans and adapt them to support your curriculum objectives or visit sites to select those appropriate for your class. You have no choice but prepare in order to help your students become responsible user of the Internet.

6. **Low Income Groups**: According to the US Department of Education, over 50% of public schools with a high minority enrollment had a lower rate of Internet access than public schools with a low minority enrollment in 1997. The same was true of instructional rooms in those schools. In addition, students from low-income families may not have computers at home or may have computers but have no access to the Internet. Consequently, students in low-income communities may be disadvantaged. To reduce the effect that social or economic status may have, you should give Internet assignments that students can easily complete while in school. If necessary, schools may need to keep computer labs open for longer and/ or during odd hours. The use of computers at public libraries should also be encouraged.

Figure 2-1: Library of Congress home page.

7. Lack of Student-Teacher Interaction:

If you stand in front of a class, then you can easily recognize by their facial expressions students who don't understand certain aspects of the lesson. When this happens, you can go back and re-explain the points to these students. Similarly, students can, through your body language or the tone of your voice, guess the main points of the lesson. Unfortunately, this personal touch is not available if the course is online.

8. New Administrative Responsibilities:

Teaching using the Internet brings to bear a new set of administrative demands on the teacher and the school administration. These include development and implementation of acceptable use policy, training, developing new evaluation criteria as needed, accreditations concerns, and addressing parents' concerns. It is also your responsibility to make sure the students receive proper training in the effective use of search engines, and on how to properly evaluate Internet materials.

2.3 Key to a Successful Use of the Internet for Teaching

Teaching using the Internet does not, by itself, lead to achieving curriculum objectives. According to studies reported in U.S. News and World Report, what makes the difference is how the Internet is actually used in the classroom. Listed below are some of the factors that are essential for a successful use of the Internet in teaching.

1. **Knowledge and Usage of the Internet and its services**: Many Internet projects require students to communicate with students from different states or countries via electronic mail or mailing lists or other news groups. According to the Chattanooga Times of December 12, 1996, most teachers cannot navigate the Internet effectively. To successfully use the Internet for teaching, you must know how to access the various services available through the Internet. Apart from assisting you in class preparation, a good knowledge of the Internet allows you to assist your students in their class activities involving the Internet.

   In addition, it has been reported that the majority of teachers who use the Internet in teaching are those who believe the Internet is a new way for doing things. These teachers also use the Internet for shopping, banking, and looking for mortgage rates. I encourage you to do so.

2. **Training on a continual basis**: You have to know
   the subject matter in order to teach your students.
   Since the Internet is a dynamic medium, you must
   train on a continual basis to effectively meet your
   students' needs regarding their Internet activities.
   A study commissioned by the American
   Association of School Administrators in 1997
   found that computer training is essential for
   effective use of technology in the classroom. Do
   not be surprised if some of your students know
   more about the Internet than you do. You should
   not shy away from learning from others, even from
   your students.

3. **Availability of equipment and technical
   assistance**: During the different Internet
   workshops I have conducted, teachers told stories
   of computer boxes in their classrooms that had

not been opened for six months or more. Some lamented about having to set up Internet wiring in their classrooms by themselves, and of having to wait for six months or more before hardware problem requests are addressed. These are not environments for effective use of technology in the classroom. In addition to buying the equipment, the school or school system should employ a computer teacher who can answer questions on curricular issues and software usage, and a technical assistant who can address hardware or software hitches.

4. **Supportive administration**: The administration should be willing to provide time and money for in-service training, employment of a computer teacher, and for purchasing equipment. They should help in a positive way in solving some of the problems that may arise as a result of your using the Internet as a tool in your classroom.

5. **Collaboration with other teachers:** You should collaborate with other teachers in the school and in the system. Cooperation and mutual understanding is important, especially when the school has few Internet accounts.

6. **Advanced planning**: *A teacher who does not plan on how to teach a given lesson is planning to fail,* to paraphrase a popular statement. You should visit the Internet to look for sites, evaluate materials, and choose appropriate sites for your class. This

way you can be sure that the resources from the site support your curriculum goals.

7. **Efficient use of technology**: Students should be trained to use available technology efficiently. For example, if you require your students to join a mailing list, then they must be trained to use e-mail efficiently and ethically.

8. **Using the Internet as a Tool**: The Internet should be a part of an integrated teaching system. It should be seen as a tool that supports and enhances learning, and not as a means by itself. A poll result conducted by Global Strategy in April 1997 shows that this is the only way the Internet adds value to the learning process.

9. **Responsible use of the Internet**: You should help your students become responsible users of the Net. Information obtained from the Net should be critically evaluated and compared with other sources. In searching the Net, the student should always have in mind the objectives and goals of the project and avoid unnecessary deviations to irrelevant sites.

10. **Provision of Web sites and Search Tools**: You should provide your students with search engines to use for their searches. For example, you can restrict the students to only search engines especially designed for educational use; you could restrict the number of search engines to be used;

or you can restrict the sites to be visited to only educational and government sites.

11. **Appropriate and exciting projects:** Internet assignments or projects should not be over complicated, boring or too demanding. They should be creative and exciting.

12. **Genuine Interest in the Process:** It is my opinion that no one, including you, should be forced to use the Internet, or any particular technology for teaching. If a teacher has no genuine interest in the process, it is likely that the teacher will not use the Internet effectively in teaching. In the long run, the students are going to be the victims. We should not allow this to happen.

13. **Good Reward System:** As pointed out earlier, it takes a lot of preparation time to effectively use the Internet for teaching. There should be evidence that the teachers' activities will be rewarded.

14. **Evaluation Method:** If you use the Internet for teaching, how would you assess students' progress? You should develop an appropriate evaluation method for your class. This is particularly important if you get your students involved in collaborative projects over which you have no direct supervision.

15. Adoption of an acceptable use policy: You should abide strictly to the letter of the acceptable use policy you have for your class. Some schools or school systems have developed acceptable use policies for teachers in their jurisdictions. If your school or system has one, use it. If not, it is imperative that you develop one for your class. In the appendix, you will find sample acceptable use policy statements that you can customize for your class.

Chapter 3

Internet Activities Appropriate For Educational Use

Not all lessons can be incorporated into the Internet. In teaching using the Net, you have to convince yourself that using the Net adds something new, some real value, to your teaching. The following are some areas where the Net has the potential to enhance your lesson.

3.1 Communication and Collaboration Activities

The Net offers a tremendous potential for learning in the area of communication and collaboration. Through the net, students can communicate or collaborate with other students or experts in the field, across geographical boundaries. An example of an expert service is "Ask Dr. Math" (http://www.mathforum.org). Students can also join a news group on a particular topic of interest. What is most interesting about the Net, as far as communication is concerned, is that it is race, age, and gender blind. So every student can benefit from a Net communication project.

3.2 Visualization and Animation Activities

If the lesson can benefit from animation, pictures, maps, and images, then the Internet could be used to support it.

For example, in studying the continent of Africa, to which the student has never been, a virtual tour to some of the countries and landmarks through the Internet will make the lesson more real. In studying some rare species of animal, it might be possible to see how the animal sounds, runs, or eats, through an animated image of the animal on the Internet. Such visualization is more likely to excite interest in the lesson than still pictures in a traditional textbook.

3.3   Re-enforcement of Class Activities

There are many interactive programs on the Internet that could be used to re-enforce lessons from the classroom. Suppose your class is studying space exploration. After the lesson, your students can go to the NASA site (http://www.nasa.gov/) to view:

1. Animated pictures of space-craft
2. An astronaut speaking from space
3. Listen to the famous speech made by J. F. Kennedy which spurred the space race

Another example, suppose your class is studying fractions or geometry. After the lesson your students can go to interactive math sites on the Internet to play math games that relate to the lesson. For example, they can visit the site: http://www.utc.edu/~cpmawata/. On this site they could play games involving fractions. They could also see animated pictures of geometric concepts such as the proof of the Pythagorean theorem. Your students could be learning math and having fun at the same time. This is the dream of every math teacher I have ever met.

Figure 3-1: Animated picture of astronaut talking from space.
http://spaceflight.nasa.gov/history/apollo/apollo11/index.html

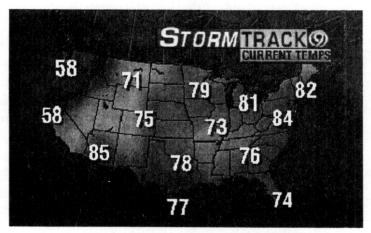

Figure 3-2. Page updated every three minutes. Web-site:
www.newschannel9.com. Reprinted with permission of Channel 9.

3.4   Current Data and Data Analysis

One of the drawbacks of a standard textbook is the 'old nature' of some data. In some instances, the data have no more intrinsic value by the time the textbook finally appears in the marketplace. The Net allows the teacher to incorporate current data into the lesson plan. This might be a current opinion poll, the current population in a given city, the current migration rate, the current weather conditions of a city on a weekly basis, or the fluctuation in the stock market. On page 25 is a current temperature of the United States of America on June 18, 2001.

3.5 Publishing and Writing Activities

The Net enables students to publish project findings to be seen by their peers around the world. This might give some students the motivation needed to complete their work on time, to be mindful of their language, and to have the sense of ownership that the traditional essay assignment may not give. Recently, a junior high school student from South Carolina sent an e-mail to me with a Web site address. When I visited the site, I saw that the student had displayed a project he had done about Botswana. Obviously, this student feels good about this project, and has some sense of ownership of it. And because he was conscious that many might view it, he took time and care in completing the project to the best of his ability. Most of the students in your classes are likely to feel good about Internet publishing, as this student was.

Figure 3-3: This page is the work of a high school student named Mark Kostreva. Reprinted with permission.

3.6   Research Resources

Compared to the library, the amount of resources available on the Internet is enormous. They continue to increase at a very rapid rate. There are millions of resources available on the Internet, which can not be found in many local libraries. This means that resources that were hard to come by and out of the reach of many are now available at minimal cost, at times free, on the Internet. For an example, the Mormon Church has been keeping data on family history for years but not many people had access to it. When it provided the service online on May 24, 1999, millions of people jammed the site, which had to be temporary closed down since it couldn't handle the traffic volume. This is a good example of how the Internet can bring scarce and unique resources to every doorstep. You may want to encourage your students to use the Internet for research if your lesson can benefit from the vast resources on the Internet.

This site can be accessed at www.lds.org.

Part II

Efficient Search and Preservation of Internet Resources

The Internet is a major tool for educational activities such as research. Carrying out research using the Internet requires the use of search tools to locate different sources of information. However, it is difficult to navigate the Internet without wasting a great deal of time in the process. To derive any substantial benefit in using the Internet for research, you have to learn to search effectively for information on your research topic. When you finally find the needed information, you must preserve it properly and use it in a responsible manner. Now that the use of the Internet is on the rise in the average American household, educators must help the general public become responsible users of the Internet. In Chapter 4 we discuss different search strategies and how to assist children to search effectively. How to preserve Internet materials efficiently is discussed in Chapter 5.

Chapter 4

EFFECTIVE USE OF SEARCH TOOLS FOR RESEARCH

Does this sound familiar? You go to the Internet to find a piece of information. After selecting your favorite search tool and typing a key word or phrase, you tell the search tool to go and find the requested information by clicking on *search*, *go find* or something similar. After a few seconds of waiting, a list of about one million sites appears on the screen. Each of the sites may also have a lead to where you may find similar or related information, depending on the search tool you use. If you do as many people do, you read the brief summary of each site, and if you suspect it has the information you need, you follow the hyperlink to the site and spend a few minutes browsing through the site to find the needed information. If you are lucky, the information on the site is exactly what you wanted, and you are done. If you are not lucky, the site doesn't contain exactly what you needed, and you have to go back to the main list and start looking for the "golden" site again. At times, when visiting a site from the main list, you meander to other sites and, once in a while, get lost. By this time you are exasperated.

As the above scenario suggests, it is difficult to navigate the Internet without getting lost or without wasting a great deal of time in the process. To derive any substantial benefit in using the Internet for research, you have to learn to search effectively for information. When you finally find the needed information, you must properly preserve and use it in a responsible manner. The purpose of this chapter is to help you search the Internet for information in a responsible and effective manner. How to access a Web site in a fast and efficient manner is also discussed. We start with an overview of Internet search tools.

4.1 Search Tools for the Internet

The Internet may be considered the ultimate library. All the information in this library is electronic in nature, and hence the Internet may be termed the *electronic library* (e-library). Unlike the school library or the one downtown, information in the e-library is not catalogued in any order. If you know the exact address of a piece of information, you can go to its location in the e-library and pick it up by typing the address in the open location of your web browser. If you don't know the exact address of the item or you need to find many places where there are references to the item, then you have to use specialized programs called *Internet Search Tools* to solve your problem. Search tools organize the resources on the Internet so that you can easily find them. There are three types of search tools, classified according to how they conduct searches on the Internet. They are Search Engines, Directory Services, and Metacrawlers.

SEARCH ENGINE
This is a software program that keeps track of all the sites on the Internet. After you type a keyword, the search engine goes to the Internet and brings back all sites that it finds containing the keyword. In conducting a keyword search, many keywords can be typed in the keyword space at the same time. In some cases, the search engine can suggest additional keywords to quicken the search.

Advanced search techniques are also available in some search engines. You should use a search engine to look for general information about a specific topic. For example, finding information on **pop music**. Some of the search engines include inforseek.com and hotbot.com. Others are given in the resources section of this chapter.

DIRECTORY SERVICE

A search tool, such as Yahoo, is called a directory service. It consists of a huge database of information that is updated regularly. The information is divided into well-defined categories, and each general category has subcategories. To initiate a search, choose a category, then narrow your search by selecting subcategories. Continue the process until the required information is found.

You should use a directory service when looking for a company, an individual, or when looking for a general category of information. Most directory services have contracts with search engines so that keyword searches can be conducted in directory services as well.

METACRAWLERS

Metacrawlers, such as **webcrawler.com**, crawl very fast through the Internet to retrieve information. Others, such as **metacrawler.com** or **infind.com**, conduct searches on the databases of major directory services. Their results are better organized and easy to understand. They are good alternatives to the search engines.

Remark: In everyday usage, the word "search engine" refers to the real search engines, the directory services, and the metacrawlers. Although a misnomer, we shall follow this usage in this book, unless there is a reason to be more specific.

4.2   Strategies for Effective Search

The skill to conduct a good search is acquired through practice and experience. There is a definite learning curve. In addition to practice and experience, formulating a concise key phrase is another factor that facilitates an effective search. It is important that you take time to process your thoughts and know exactly what you want to find before calling on the search engine to perform a search for you. Some of the other factors that can assist you in an effective search of the Internet are given below.

General Techniques

1. Different search engines search the Internet differently. Use as many search engines as possible for your search.
2. There are many services that rate search engines (see the resources section). Find out how each search engine is rated. This will give you some degree of reliability on the results of the search engine you use.
3. Before choosing a search engine, find out how it conducts a search or indexes sites. A good understanding of how a search engine works will help you perform an effective search.
4. On each search engine is a "How to" page, or a similar phrase. Read this page to learn about how to conduct an effective search using your chosen search engine.
5. Below the results of some search are "Try this" or "More like this" messages. Look at these sites also. It is possible to find better information on these sites than on the one listed.

6. Be mindful of your spelling. If the results of your search look strange, check your spelling. Nobody is above this particular mistake!

7. Tell the search engine exactly what you want. If you are looking for a "man from space," then it is better to use that phrase first rather than using "space" or "man." It is important to be precise in the wording of your key phrase.

Advanced Search Techniques

1. Use the search options or Advanced Search Techniques provided by the search engine. This allows you to use the special syntax used by that particular search engine. Different search engines may use slightly different syntax.

2. Use quotes. If you use the key phrase **pop music**, most search engines will return sites containing *pop* or *music* or both. However, if your key phrase is enclosed in quotes, **"pop music,"** it returns only sites containing both **pop** and **music**.

3. Specify words that must appear by putting a plus, (+), in front of the word, with no spaces. For example, +airline+ticket tells the search engine that all hits must contain *airline* and *ticket*.

4. Specify words that must not appear by putting a minus sign (-) in front of the word, with no spaces. For example, +boy-moose. This tells the search engine that the word *boy* must appear but *moose* must not appear in the results.

5. Use Boolean operators: AND, OR, NOT. For example, **pop AND music** means that all hits must contain the words pop and music; **pop OR music** means a document that contains any of the two words should be returned; and **pop NOT**

music means that all hits must contain *pop* but not *music*. (If the search engine doesn't accept **pop NOT music** try **pop AND NOT music**.)
6. Specify a publication date, if possible. Using the advanced search techniques, you can specify the publication date or the period of time in which the material was published in some search engines.
7. Specify the language. Some search engines allow you to specify the language in which the document must appear, to eliminate documents in languages you cannot read.
8. Specify location or domain. This feature allows you to specify the region, country, or continent from which the sites should come. For example, rather than look for pop music from sites all over the world, you can specify if the site containing it is located in a server in the United States. Moreover, this feature allows you to limit the sites to educational sites (edu), government sites (gov), or as appropriate for your needs.
9. Specify the type of media. This is another advanced technique in most search engines. You can use the option to exclude sites containing media technology that your computer cannot handle. Such media technologies include Java, MP3, Shockwave, VRML, Real Player, Active X, and Win Media.

Demonstration

In this section, we illustrate how to effectively search the Internet using the different Internet search tools. Suppose we want information on *pop music*.

Using the HotBot Search Engine: http://www.hotbot.lycos.com/

Key Phrase	Number of Hits	Comments
1. Pop music	More than100,000	Get sites containing pop or music or both.
2. "Pop music"	More than 10,000	Get sites containing both pop and music.
3. "Music pop"	Greater than 5,000.	Note that order is important when using quotes.
4. +music+pop	More than 500,000	
5. +music-pop	More than 10,000	

Remarks:

   a. Note that by using quotes the number of sites listed in Item 2 is less than that of Item 1 by at least 90,000.

   b. Observe that Item 5 has at least 490,000 fewer hits than Item 4.

Searching Using Yahoo! Directory Service: http://www.yahoo.com

Figure 4-1: Yahoo.com website. Reproduced with permission of Yahoo! Inc. © 2000 by Yahoo! Inc. Yahoo and the Yahoo! logo are trademarks of Yahoo! Inc.

1. Select **the music category** under entertainment.
2. Many subcategories can be chosen from the menu that appears. Let us select the **history** subcategory.
3. There are now seven more sub-subcategories to choose from. Suppose you are not sure which of them to choose. To search for *pop music* in all the remaining subcategories, type *pop music* into the keyword space, check the **just this category** box and click **search**.
4. The search results in zero categories and 33 sites for pop music. You can now go through each site to look for the information you need.

Searching Using MetaCrawler.com

1. Type *pop music* into the keyword space and check the **all option** box. (By checking this option, you are asking the metacrawler to search all search engines in its database.) Click **search**.
2. There are only 75 sites for pop music. Notice that the number of hits is small compared to what you had using a search engine or directory service.
3. Click on **back** to get to the previous page and select **power search**. The menu that appears gives options such as the search engine to use, how you want to view your results or the location and domain you want to search from.
4. For the purpose of our demonstration, suppose you check **relevance** under view results, select **AltaVista** as the search engine to use, and **North America** under the domain and location submenu. And then click on **search**.
5. There are 10 sites found for this power search.

Remarks: Please use power search only when you know exactly where to find the information. If you have to use a power search, it is a good idea not to limit the number of search engines to use, unless there is a good reason for doing so.

4.3   Helping School Children Search Effectively

Figure 4 - 2: Search results displayed by MetaCrawler.com

According to *The Condition of Education 98*, Indicator 4, more than 78 percent of public schools in the United States have Internet access. Moreover, the number of households having Internet access is steadily increasing as cheaper personal computers are getting to the market. To fully realize the educational benefits of the Internet for our children and students, adults have the moral obligation of ensuring responsible use. The following list gives suggestions on how you can help children search the Internet effectively.

1. Instill in your children the habit of using the search engines efficiently as suggestive earlier in this chapter. Give assignments that require them to search rationally for information on the Internet. Ask each of them to explain why he/she thinks the search was effective.
2. Not all information on the Internet is accurate. Establish criteria that your children or students should use to validate their information. Efforts should be made to ensure that each child uses the Internet in a sensible way.
3. Searching the Web can be overwhelming and distracting. It is not uncommon for adults to get lost and waste an enormous amount of time on the Internet. Give children the sites or key phrases to use in their searches. This might not be necessary for older children, but it is certainly a must for the younger ones.
4. There are search engines that are specifically designed for children or for educational use. Please encourage your children to use these types of search engines.
5. There are some sites that assemble or index other children's sites or educational sites. Try using these sites, which are listed under repository sites at the end of this chapter.
6. You must have an Acceptable Use Policy (AUP) if you are helping children use the Internet. The AUP should spell out in clear language what your expectations are and the consequences of not towing the line. Moreover, have a plan for dealing with children who abuse these policies. Make sure that the AUP is fully enforced when the need

arises. You should ask parents to sign the AUP statement. (See examples of AUP in the Appendix.)

7. When you give children any research assignment, make sure they understand exactly what you want from them. A carefully worded research assignment can help children to search wisely, stay out of bad sites, and make your work easier in the long run.

8. There are many sites on the Internet that are not appropriate for children. Minimize access to inappropriate materials by using filtering software.

4.4 Faster and Efficient Access to Internet Sites

Loading a Web page can take a long time, especially if you are using a dial-up connection, because browsers automatically load all available features that will help them interpret the Web page properly. Unfortunately, loading some of these features is slow and wastes valuable time during research projects. However, Internet browsers do have some mechanisms which allow you to turn off these features so that your Internet access is faster and less frustrating. We discuss these features and how to turn them off below.

Do not display Images

Loading pictures takes a long time. You can disable this feature by following the steps on page 41:

In Netscape:
1. On the **Edit** menu, click on **Preferences**.
2. In the preference window, choose **Advance** category.
3. Uncheck the **Automatically Load Images** box.
4. Click **OK** to exit preferences.

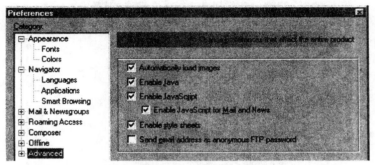

Figure 4 - 3: Turning off media devices in Netscape browser.

Remarks: To see pictures after disabling the Automatic Image Load feature, click on the picture icon and select the **Automatic Load Images** box under preferences.

In Explorer
1. Open the **Tools** menu in the toolbar and click on **Internet Options**.
2. Select the **Advanced** category.
3. In the **Multimedia** area, clear one or more of the options: **Show pictures, Play animations, Play videos,** or **Play sounds** if the boxes are checked.

Remarks:
1. To see a picture or animation after clearing **Show pictures** or **Play videos** options, right-click on its icon and then click **Show Picture**.

2. Click **refresh** in the **View** menu to hide any picture on the current page that is still visible after you cleared the **Show pictures** check box.

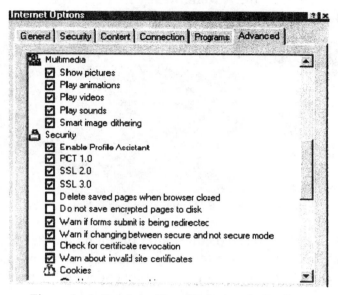

Figure 4 - 4: Turning off media devices in Explorer.

Start with no home page

When you start a browser, it first loads its home page or the one you specify. You can get to the Internet site that you want faster by instructing the browser not to load any home page. Follow the steps below to enable this feature.

In Netscape:

1. On the **Edit** menu of the browser, click on **Preferences**.

2. In the preference window, choose the **Navigator** category.

3. In the **Navigator Starts with** box, select **Blank Page or Last Page visited** option.
4. Click **OK** to exit preferences.

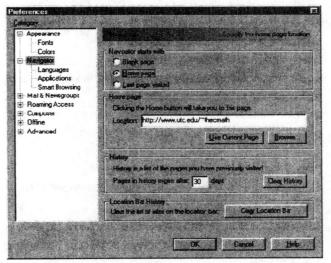

Figure 4 - 5: How to start Netscape without loading the first page.

In Explorer:
1. Open the **View** menu in the toolbar and click on **Internet Options**.
2. Select the **General** category.
3. In the **Home Page** box, select **Use Blank**.
4. Click **OK** to exit and save the newly chosen option.

Caching Web Pages

When you visit a Web site using Netscape browser or Internet Explorer, your computer caches or stores the Web pages in the memory cache or the disk cache. If you have to visit the page again, the browser loads it from your hard drive. The loading is very fast since it is coming from your hard drive. By clicking the **reload** button, you can go to the real Internet site again to check for updates.

The number of pages cached depends on the memory size available to the browser. To increase the memory size, follow the steps below:

In Netscape Navigator
1. On the **Edit** menu of the browser, click on **Preferences**.
2. In the preference window, choose the **Advance** category. If the advanced category window does not contain the cache option, click on the sign (+) beside the advanced category window.

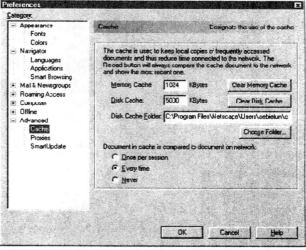

Figure 4 - 6: How to increase cache memory in Netscape.

3. Select **Cache**.
4. If setting the cache memory, specify the size you want in the memory cache field.
   If setting the disk cache, specify the size you want in the disk cache field.

In Internet Explorer
1. On the **Tools** menu, choose **Internet Options**.
2. In the **Temporary Internet File** box, click on **Settings**.
3. In the **Temporary Internet File Folder** box, there is a slider, which asks for the amount of disk space to use as a percentage of the amount of space in the hard drive. Move the slider to the right to increase cache size.
4. Click on **OK** twice to save the setting.

Remark: Under settings, you can also specify when Explorer can update the pages.

Remark: A size of 7680K is recommended for disk cache, and a size of 1024K to 2000K is recommended for memory cache. Under settings, you can also specify when Navigator can update the pages.

Clearing the Disk Cache

The cache can get full easily, depending on the number of sites visited and the number of pages in each site. You can improve the browser's performance by emptying the cache on a regular basis. Follow these steps to clear the content of the cache:

In Netscape:
1. On the **Edit** menu, click on **Preferences**.
2. In the preferences, choose the **Advance** category. If the advanced category window does not contain the cache option, click on the sign (+) beside the advanced category

3. Select **Cache**.
4. Click on the **clear disk cache** button and on the **clear memory cache** button.
5. Click **OK**.

In Internet Explorer
1. On the **Tools** menu, choose **Internet Options**.
2. In the **Temporary Internet File** box, click **Delete Files**.
3. In the **Delete Files** window, click on **OK**.
4. Click **OK** again to exit Internet Options.

Remark: See figures 4-5 and 4-6.

4.5 Resources for Effective Search of the Internet

Internet resources that may help you search are listed below. This list is not exhaustive, and since the Internet is a dynamic medium, these sites may change without notice and new ones are likely to be created.

Search engines tutorials and rating services

1. **Search Engine Watch**
   http://www.searchenginewatch.com
   This site gives an overview of the major search engines, information on specialty search services, and ratings of search engines. A tutorial on how to conduct an effective search is also available.
2. **SearchInternet.com**
   http://search.internet.com
   This site provides search tips and power search capability. It works best when you use descriptive

phrases as opposed to keywords. For example, it does a better search if you type "drivers for Sanyo 40X- CDR hard drive " than just "hard drive" or "drivers."

3. **Spiders Apprentice**
   http://www.monash.com/spidap.html
   This site provides information on how you can search the Web more efficiently. It also gives a comprehensive ranking of most of the search engines

4. **Search Engine Showdown**
   http://www.notess.com/search/
   This is one of the most comprehensive search engine references on the Internet. It has a chart comparing the search engines and their capabilities. Most importantly, it has good basic suggestions for how to search the Web and when to use each of the search tools.

5. **Microsoft Insider**
   http://www.msn.com/tutorial/default.html
   This site provides a comprehensive guide to the Internet and Web tutorials.

6. **ICONnect-Advanced Online Courses**
   http://www.ala.org/ICONN/advancedcourses.html
   This is an online course on how to use e-mail.

Searching in the Classroom, Kids Safe Resources

7. **Lycos Zone**
   http://www.lycos.com/kids/
   This site provide resources for teachers and parents under the teacher zone and family zones, respectively.

8. **The Web Guide for Kids**
   http://www.yahooligans.com
   This is a one-stop site for students, teachers and parents.

9. **NPAC Web Site**
   http://www.npac.syr.edu:80/Education/index.html
   NPAC prepares and deliver computer sciences courses that spans K-12 curriculum and continue education programs.

10. **Internet Cyber Patrol**
    http://www.cyberpatrol.com
    This site provides surf control and cyber patrol software that meet the needs of homes, education and business.

11. **Net Nanny**
    http://www.netnanny.com/
    The net nanny software should provide around the clock protection for your children as the surf the Internet.

12. **Yahoo Education Directory**
    http://www.yahoo.com/Education/
    This is a repository site for educational materials and online learning communities. You can also request Yahoo to post your educational materials on the site.

13. **Eisenhower National Clearinghouse**
    http://www.enc.org
    The mission of ENC is to "identify effective curriculum resources, create high-quality professional development materials, and disseminate useful information and products to improve K-12 mathematics and science teaching and learning."

14. **Classroom Connect**

    http://www.classroom.net

    Resources for K-12 teachers and their students are provided on this site. They provide a forum where you can share ideas, ask experts, discover the best new teaching resources, engage in online collaborative projects, and help each other integrate technology into the classroom. You must sign up to be a member in order to be provided with these benefits.

14. **Education World.**

    http://www.education-world.com

    This sites claims to be the educator's best friend. Lesson plans, sites reviews and search engines that search only educational sites are provided.

15. **Awesome Library:**

    http://www.awesomelibrary.org/

    This site collects and organizes reviewed educational materials and sites. The site is very safe for kids.

16. **Learning Network: Fact Monster**

    http://kids.infoplease.com/

    There are many activities for children at this site, which they can use to re-enforce classroom lessons.

17. **Kids Click**

    http://sunsite.berkeley.edu/KidsClick!/

    Kids click is a site for kids created by the Ramapo Catskill Library System and maintained by the Colorado State Library. One of the distinguishing features of this site is that it is free of advertisements.

18. **Study WEB**

    http://www.studyweb.com

    This site, which is only available through school subscription, provides online activities that are tailored state and national standards.

19. Kids Search Tools
http://www.rcls.org/ksearch.htm
Tools for kids search are provided at this site. You can also search the Merriam-Webster Collegiate Dictionary, Merriam-Webster Collegiate Thesaurus, Encarta, and the 6th edition of the Columbia encyclopedia directly from the site.

Search Engines
1. http://www.search.com
2. http://www.lycos.com
3. http://www.altavista.digital.com
4. http://www.excite.com
5. http://www.hotbot.com
6. http://www.northernlight.com
7. http://www.infoseek.com.
8. http://www.goto.com/
9. http://affiliate.directhit.com

Directory Services
1. http://www.yahoo.com
2. http://www.looksmart.com
3. http://a2z.lycos.com
4. http://search.netscape.com
5. http://search.excite.com
6. http://nscp.snap.com/
7. http://search.about.com/
8 http://www.google.com/

Metacrawlers
1. http://www.webcrawler.com
2. http://www.metacrawler.com
3. http://www.infind.com

Filtering Software for Kids

These allow blocking of sites containing indecent materials.
1. http://www.security-online.com/info/filtering.html
2. http://www.netnanny.com/netnanny/
3. http://www.safesurf.com/
4. http://www.mhonline.net/starting/safesurf.htm
5. http://www.integrityinternet.com/

Search Engines with Filter for Kids

1. Ask Jeeves For Kids:
    http://www.ajkids.com/
2. Disney Internet Guide (DIG):
    http://www.disney.com/dig/today/
3. Yahooligans: http://www.yahooligans.com/
4. AltaVista Family Filter:
    http://www.altavista.com/
5. Lycos SafetyNet:
    http//personal.lycos.com/safetynet/
    safetynet.asp
6. Searchopolis:
    http://www.searchopolis.com/

Browsers
1. **Microsoft Explorer**
    http://www.microsoft.com/windows/ie/default.asp

2. **Netscape Communicator**
    http://home.netscape.com/ex/shak/shopping/
    index.html

Reference
National Center for Education Statistics (1988). Internet Access in Public Schools in *The Condition of Education 1998, Indicator 4*

http://nces.ed.gov/pubs98/condition98/c9804a01.html
(January 2000).

Chapter 5

EFFICIENT PRESERVATION OF INTERNET RESOURCES

You have found some information on the Internet that relates to your project. How do you preserve this information so that you can use it for research anytime you want? What can you do so that you can get back to the site in the most convenient way?

We recommend that you get this information, or its Uniform Resource Locator (URL), from the Internet and preserve it locally. There are many advantages for this. First, it gives you time to rigorously evaluate each resource for usability as suggested in Chapter 6. Second, you do not tie up the access account, the phone line or make the

Internet go sluggish due to overuse. Third, if your account has limited access time, it becomes more imperative to get materials from the Internet quickly and then preserve them locally where you can access them without *external* time limitation. Finally, preserving the URL enables you to get back to the site without delay. The following are ways in which you can preserve materials obtained from the Internet:

5.1   Whacking the Web site
A Web whacker program, such as www.bluesquirrel.com, or a similar program, 2ndSite, allows you to download the Web pages or the entire Web site, including links and images, onto your local hard drive. This enables you to view the site, even on computers with no Internet connections, away from the Internet and at your convenience. It is an ideal situation for presentation where there is no Internet connection or for making the Internet available to those with no Internet connection. Since the pages are coming from your local hard drive, loading is pretty fast. If you consider using a Web whacker program, you must have a good sized hard drive, since the program downloads everything including images and links. Also note that you have to buy and learn to use the program efficiently in order to derive maximum benefit from it.

5.2   Bookmark or Favorite Folder
Internet browsers allow you to create a folder and store the URL of a site that you visit or want to visit regularly. By marking a Web site, you avoid the problem of remembering and typing some lengthy URL. This folder is called *bookmark* in Netscape and *favorite* in Explorer.

In Netscape:

1. Open the page you want to add to your bookmark folder.
2. When the document loading is done, open the **Bookmark** menu and select **Add Bookmark**. The page is now added to your bookmark folder.

In Explorer:

3. Open the page you want to add to your collection of favorite pages.
4. When the document loading is done, open the **Favorites menu**, and select **Add to Favorites.**
5. Type a new name for the page if you want to.
6. Click **Create In** to choose a folder to place the favorite site or create a new folder for it.

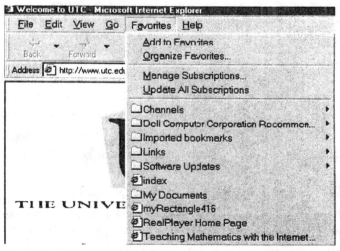

Figure 5-1: Favorite Menu in Explorer

To open a marked page:
1. Click the **Bookmark** button on the toolbar,
2. Open the folder containing the marked page, if it is in a folder.
3. Double click on the name of page you want to open.

5.3   Saving Web Pages
You can save the content of a Web page or any portion of it on your local hard drive or a floppy disk so that you can view it without going to the Internet. Note that the browsers only save the text and not the graphics.

In Netscape:
1. Open the **File** menu, and click **Save As**.
2. On the window that appears, double click on the folder you want the page to be saved in.
3. In the **File Name** box, type a name for the page.
4. In the **Save as type** box, select the format you want.
5. Click **Save** or **OK** to conclude the process

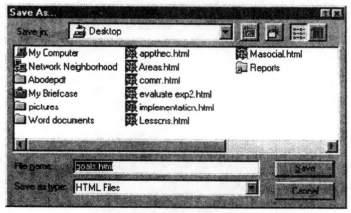

Figure 5 - 2: The save dialog boxes in Netscape

In Explorer:
1. On the **File** menu, click **Save As**.
2. Double-click the folder you want to save the page in.
3. In the **File Name** box, type a name for the page.
4. In the **Save as type** box, select the format you want.
5. In the **Language** box, select the language type.
6. Click **Save** or **OK** to conclude the process.

To save a picture or other graphic

In Netscape:
1. Place the cursor on the image and right-click on the mouse.
2. On the menu that appears, click **Save Image As**.
3. In the **File Name** box, type a name for the image or picture.
4. In the **Save as type** box, select the format you want.
5. Click **Save** or **OK** to conclude the process

In Explorer:

1. Place cursor on picture and right-click on the mouse
2. On the menu that appears, click **Picture As**.
3. In the **File Name** box, type a name for the image.
4. In the **Save as type** box, select the format you want.
5. Click **Save** or **OK** to conclude the process.

Figure 5 - 3: Save dialogue in Explorer

5.4 Copying information from a Web page into a document

You can also preserve information from a Web page by copying the information directly into an open document that you are working on, or by storing it in a disk.

In Netscape and Explorer:

1. Select the image or the portion of the information you want to copy.
2. (To copy the text of an entire pages, click the **Edit** menu, and then click **Select All**.)
3. On the **Edit** menu, click **Copy**.
4. Make active the document where you want the image or information to appear. Click the location where you want to place it.
5. On the **Edit** menu in that document, click **Paste**.

5.5 Printing Web Pages

It may be necessary at times to print and keep a hard copy of a Web page so that you can use it later, share it with people with no computers, or use it for evaluation in an environment with no computers. There are many options to printing a Web page. We will talk about printing the page as you see it on the screen. The browsers allow you to specify some of the information you need printed such as the page URL, page numbers, and window title.

In Netscape:

To print the contents of the current window

Click on the **print button** of the toolbar; or
On the **File** menu, click **Print.**

To change how a page looks when it prints

1. On the **File** menu, click **Page Setup.**
2. In **Margins** boxes, type the margin measurements in approximate units: inches in USA.
3. In the **Page option box** area, select the page option of your choice.
4. In the **Headers box,** indicate if you want the document title or the URL printed
5. In the **Footers box**, indicate if you want page numbers, page totals or date printed to be shown.
6. Click **OK** and exit page setup.
7. Click on **Print** in the file menu or on the toolbar to print the document according to your format.

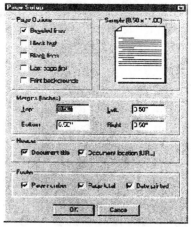

Figure 5 - 4: Netscape Page-up dialog box

In Explorer:

To print the contents of the current window

1. Click on the **print button** of the toolbar; or On the **File** menu, click on **Print**.
2. Set the printing options you want.
3. Click **OK** to print the document.

To change how a page looks when it prints

1. Open the **File** menu, and click on **Page Setup**.
2. In the **Paper Box**, select the paper size and the printing source.
3. In the **Margins** boxes, type the measurements in appropriate units: inches for USA.
4. In the **Orientation** box, select either **Portrait** or **Landscape** to specify whether you want the page printed vertically or horizontally, respectively.
5. In the **Headers** and **Footers** boxes, specify the information to be printed by using the following variables (can be combined with text).

To print this	Enter this
Window title	&w
Page address (URL)	&u
Date in short format(as specified)	&d
Date in long format (as specified)	&D
Time in the format specified	&t
Time in 24-hour format	&T
Current page number	&p
Total number of pages	&P
Centered text (following &b)	&b
Right-aligned text (after &b&b)	&b&b
A single ampersand (&)	&&

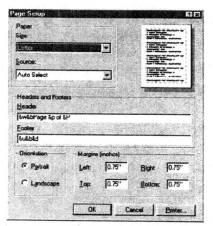

Figure 5 - 5: Explore page up dialog box

Remark: You can set the settings in centimeters. To do this, go to the Control Panel and change the Regional Settings as follows:

1. Click on **Regional Options**.
2. Select **Numbers**.
3. Under measurement, select **metric,** click on **apply**.

Figure 5 - 6: Explore regional options dialog box

Resources:

Browsers

1. **Microsoft Explorer**
   http://www.microsoft.com/windows/ie/default.asp

2. **Netscape Communicator**
   http://home.netscape.com/ex/shak/shopping/
   index.html

Part III

Evaluating Internet Materials and Projects

There are many materials and communication projects on the Internet. Since anyone with an Internet Server can post anything on the Internet, it is important that all materials or projects from the Internet be evaluated for accuracy and for meeting curriculum goals. Chapter 6 contains a template for evaluating Internet materials. How to evaluate Internet collaborative projects is discussed in Chapter 7.

Chapter 6

RESPONSIBLE USE OF
INTERNET MATERIALS

Not every piece of information found on the Internet or received by e-mail is accurate. Unfortunately, many people believe that any information that comes out from a computer is correct. This situation presents a big challenge to all of us who use the Internet for research or require others to use Internet materials in one form or the other. Consider the following true stories.

First, aspartame is an artificial sweetener used in diet products such as diet sodas. In an e-mail circulated around 1998-99, and which may still continue today, Nancy Markle claimed that aspartame causes cancer, birth defects, and diabetes, among other horrible ailments. However, according to medical literature, aspartame can only cause problems to persons with phenylketonuria, because persons with this problem lack the ability to properly absorb one of the ingredients in aspartame. But Nancy's article was silent on this real health effect of aspartame, making people believe that she was out to deceive the public or had some personal vendetta with the manufacturers or commercial users of aspartame.

Second, on August 25, 2000, 23-year old Mark Jakob posted a hoax press release on the Web site of Emulex, a data networking equipment company, which caused its stock to plummet about 62%. The hoax press release, which used the company's letter head, claimed that Emulex was under investigation by the Security and Exchange Commission, its chief executive had resigned, its 1998 and 1999 earnings had been re-stated, and that its fourth quarter earnings for 2000 had been revised from gain to loss. The unfortunate thing about the Emulex case is that the hoax news was spread through the Internet by news services. For example, Dow Jones and Bloomberg news wire services carried the news, without verifying its accuracy.

There are other sites that contain only half-truths and are meant to lure the surfer to other things. For example, a first grade teacher had a project on Australian Koala. According to her, most of the sites she found said little or nothing about Koala and were used for selling Koala T-shirts and for selling hotel reservations.

Another area of concern in using the Internet for research is propaganda. Many interest groups, some not well known or admired, can post their different viewpoints on the Internet. Most of the time, the information is biased or the truth is twisted for personal gain.

If you are using the Internet for research, how do you avoid being a victim of people like Nancy Markle or Mark Jakob? A responsible user of the Internet must be able to critically evaluate materials obtained from an Internet site or by e-mail. This evaluation process entails looking for accuracy of content as well as appropriateness for intended use.

6.1   Evaluating Internet Search Results

The materials we traditionally use in our research go through extensive evaluation processes. First, editors in the publishing firm evaluate each manuscript for content accuracy and then for clarity of presentation. Some of the manuscripts are also sent to experts in the area for independent evaluation. Only manuscripts that pass stated criteria are selected for publication. The second evaluation process is done by teachers, parents, and by other educators. On an individual basis or by committee, educators evaluate materials from publishers for appropriateness. Those meeting specific needs are selected for acquisition. Third, librarians evaluate books and other materials meant for libraries for appropriateness before acquisition.

On the other hand, nobody evaluates materials published on the Internet for accuracy, let alone for meeting specific education goals. Since anyone with access to a Web server can publish on the Internet, it is imperative that we establish criteria for evaluating Internet materials intended for educational use. Any evaluation criteria

should address, among others:
1. Accuracy and reliability;
2. Ability to meet specific education or research needs;
3. Advantage over using traditional materials.

6.2 Detailed Evaluation Criteria for Internet Materials

Accuracy and Reliability:
1. Find out the creator of the site. What are the author's qualifications for writing on this subject?
2. Find out who is the sponsor or maintainer of the site. Is the information accurate? Is the site used to propagate the sponsor's viewpoint?
3. Find out if the information is biased or not. Are you persuaded to agree on certain opinions or ideology? Are you lured to buy some items? Is it an infomercial?
4. Verify the timeliness of the content. Is the information on the site up to date? When was it last updated?
5. Find out if the site has been reviewed. If it has been reviewed, what is the rating? Did it receive any award or honorable mention? If it has not been reviewed, what makes you believe that the content is accurate and of high quality?

Education/Research Needs:
1. In what ways does the site support your specific teaching or research needs?
2. What is the site's audience? Are the materials on the site suitable for the project?

Advantage Over Traditional Material:
1. What types of Internet technologies are available at the site? How would these enhance your research project or teaching needs? Do you have the accessories needed to take full advantage of the Internet technologies that the site provides?
2. Are the related links from the site, if any, of high quality? Do they provide materials that complement the site's materials?
3. How well designed is the site? Can you find what you are looking for easily? Is it easy to navigate without being lost?

6.3   Using the Evaluation Process:

Demonstrations
In the workshops we conducted for teachers in June 1998 and 1999, we asked the teachers to evaluate Web sites of their choosing using the above criteria. Below are three such evaluations. (Please note that these sites could change or be taken off the Web in the future. However, the principle illustrated will continue to be useful.)

Demonstration 1

Evaluator: Eltis Capel, Hamilton County School System, Chattanooga, TN

Web site: http://www.richmond.edu/~ed344/96/math/

Title: What Good is Math?

Author: This site was created by Jen Peck, Karen Rosser, and Carol Pifer, students at the University of Richmond studying in the departments of Math and Education. Also, *Mathletics* pages in this document were created by Mary Beth Indelicato, a student at the University of Richmond studying in the departments of Math and Education.

Sponsor: Dr. Patricia Stohr-Hunt has maintained and revised this document as an interactive resource for educators, students and parents. All inquiries and comments regarding this document could be mailed to her by using an e-mail address given at the site.

Accuracy: The site is done by students in the Departments of Math and Education, which I would assume is for part of their grade, so it would be reasonable to assume that the information is accurate.

Bias: I feel there is no room for bias here, because the students are using factual information that doesn't change. Addition, Subtraction, Multiplication and Fractions don't change in their answers.

Timeliness: The Web site was last worked on in 1998.

However, the information is still up to date.

Awards: This site was rated "Great!" and awarded three stars in Barbara Feldman's 3/31/99 syndicated newspaper column "Surfing the Net with Kids." This column appears in the San Diego Union-Tribune.

This site was also featured in the October 1998 issue of the "Top 10 Educational Sites on the World-Wide Web." It was selected in January 1998 as one of the Internet's finest informative sites and is included in StudyWeb's listing of educational links. In October 1997, the site received a four-star rating and was awarded a Blue Web'n. It was reviewed by EducationWorld and awarded "Best of June" for 1997, receiving an "A+" Rating.

Education needs: I give this site a definite "Two-Thumbs Up." It supports my entire curriculum needs and then some. It is easy to follow and most of all "practical." Any student can see the everyday use of math in their life.

Audience: Target Audience is anyone from 2nd Grade to 12th Grade.

Internet Technologies: It uses all Internet features very well: colors, graphics, easy to get to screens, etc. I really enjoyed the site. You could leave at anytime and easily get to where you wanted to go.

Links: The Links are awesome! They are just as good as the Web site itself, if not better. I am very impressed with the links. Again, more interactive math games.

Design: It doesn't have the most sophisticated bells and whistles that are out there, but it is pleasing to the eye and children can relate to the pictures. Layout is very good. Hyperlinks are colorful, creative and imaginative. They are things we see everyday in one form or another. In conclusion, this is my two cents worth. I am very impressed with the Web site that I found.

Demonstration 2

Evaluator: Regina Tanksley, Hamilton County school System, Chattanooga, TN

Web site: http://www.dcs.edu/hasp/Butterflies/int.html.

Title: Life Cycle of the Butterfly

Author: This site, HASP - Hands-on Activity Science Program, was created by a partnership of eight school districts and the Institute for Science Education at the University of Alabama in Huntsville. All of the authors of this site are educators.

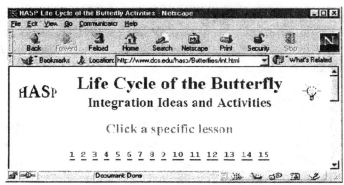

Figure 6-1: HASP Life Cycle of the Butterfly Activities Site.
Reprinted with permission

Sponsor: The Institute for Science Education at UAH and the National Science Foundation sponsor the site. The information appears to be accurate. I base this solely on the fact that I conducted this experiment, The Life Cycle of the Painted Lady Butterfly, with my kiddos this year. Sharyl Nye, HASP consultant, and the Office of Instructional Technology maintain this site.

Accuracy: This is a lesson plan. I feel that there is no bias. This plan is developed according to the teachers' expectations for the lesson/lessons. The reader is not persuaded to agree. In fact, the reader has the ability to modify this lesson according to the particular needs of their students.

Timeliness: The content is up to date. This site was last modified, according to the site, on Tuesday, June 15, 1999.

Award: There is no indication that this site has been reviewed, received a rating or any award or honorable mention. However, this site/program is supported through federally funded grants.

Education Needs: This site definitely supports my specific curriculum needs...and then some. I find this to be an awesome site! The homepage address is: http://www.dcs.edu/hasp/

Audience: The target audience is the teacher/educator (K-6)...possibly college students preparing for student teaching or those students who need assistance in getting jump started in developing a lesson plan for a college course.

Internet Technologies: This is a basic site. There is no animation, only use of pictures/graphics and graphs. It does give the date and time. Information is provided regarding curricular pages, projects, and the schools and faculty involved. The project leaders are listed with e-mail addresses, snail mail, and telephone numbers right at your fingertips.

Links: The links are easy to access within this Web page itself. The links are interrelated to science and its uses within the classroom. There are no related links to other sites on the Web within this home page. However, I find this site to be packed with a lot of science ideas/projects for the classroom.

Design: I find the site appealing. It is easy to use and not too busy. Very simple...the way that I like things...to the point and precise.

Demonstration 3

Evaluator: Wyndy Metcalf, McConnell Elementary, Chattanooga, Tennessee

Web site: http://amazing-space.stsci.edu/trading/ directions.html

Title: Collecting Solar System Trading Cards

Authors: The authors of the site are Betty McCue (Elementary Teacher at Maryland School with expertise in elementary education, computers, and enrichment), Connie Flowers (Elementary Teacher at Maryland School with expertise in elementary education and Science), Alex Storrs (Scientist at Space Telescope Science Institute with expertise in planetary science, comets, and asteroids), and Lisa Sherbert, Amy Gerimada, and Steve Drasco (Student interns and staff members at Space Telescope Science Institute)

Sponsors: This Web site is sponsored by the Space Telescope Science Institute in Maryland, and The Association of Universities for Research in Astronomy.

Bias: Information shows no bias and would appear to be reliable given the authors and site sponsors. All objectives and information from the site meet National Education Standards.

Timeliness: This site was last updated 11/8/96. While this was several years ago, the information that is contained within the site does not become out of date this quickly.
Award: While the site does not appear to have been rated or to have received an award, it has been reviewed and tested by the space Telescope Science Institute in 1996. It can be assumed that this site was also reviewed by its

other sponsor, The Association of Universities for research in Astronomy, Inc.

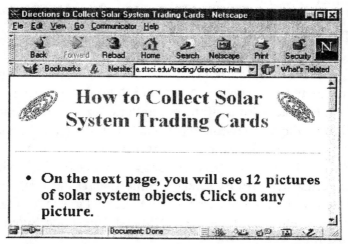

Figure 6-2: Space Telescope Solar System Trading Cards Site. This site was created for NASA by STSCI.

Curriculum Needs: Yes, this site has the information needed by my students to complete their research project. An added bonus is that they will have fun while they do it! Additionally, lesson plans for the teacher are included.

Audience: This site was designed with students, specifically 3-6 grades, and teachers in mind.

Internet Technologies: Graphics, photographs, and movies are used in the site. An added feature, however, is the on-line dictionary that is built in. When students come across a new science term, they simply click on the word for clarification.

Links: All other related sites are of high quality as well. They are also written or sponsored by reliable institutions

such as NASA, National Space Science Data Center, or other educational facilities.

Design: The site is visually interesting and engaging. Text is large, chunked, and easy to read. Graphics and other pictures are valid and used well. The site is easy to navigate with menus on each page. Gathering planet trading cards as students learn about the solar system is a clever way to motivate and pique children's interest. The directions for this site are straightforward and easy to follow.

6.4 Helping Children Evaluate Internet Materials

1. Explain to them why Internet materials must be evaluated for accuracy and why it is not necessary to evaluate materials obtained from the library.
2. Give students assignments on how to actually evaluate an Internet site. The earlier students are exposed to this idea, the better it is for them and for the helper.
3. When evaluating a site or Internet materials, the skills children should master include:

a. Mastery of evaluation criteria. You can give them these criteria as you deem fit or you can coach them to develop their own set of criteria.
b. Step-by-step evaluation of resources found on the Internet using criteria developed or the one you provided.
c. Deciding whether the material evaluated is appropriate for the project at hand. For example, why is the chosen material more appropriate for the topic than those rejected?

Remark:
Using the Internet for research requires a great deal of effort. Not only do you have to search effectively, but also you have to objectively and critically evaluate each resource. Is it worth the effort of going through these daunting tasks just for the sake of using Internet materials for research? Why not use library resources or surveys? I believe that using the Internet for research is worth all of this work. However, there are some shortcomings as pointed out in Chapter 2. The Internet should complement and not replace a good library or an encyclopedia.

References

1. ABC News (2000). Portrait of a Criminal, http://abcnews.go.com/sections/business/DailyNews/emulex_000901.html
2. Christine Gorman (1999). A web of Deceit, Time Magazine, February 8, 1999.
3. Jan Alexander and Marsha Tate (1996-1998). The Web as a Research Tool: Evaluation Techniques http://www.science.widener.edu/~withers/evaout.htm

4. The Motly Fool (2000).
   Emulex may have found its man
   http://www.fool.com/news/breakfast/2000/
   breakfast000901.htm
5. University of St. Thomas ISS-Center (1998).
   How to Evaluate a Website.
   http://www.iss.sthomas.edu/webtruth/indexhtm

Chapter 7

RESPONSIBLE INVOLVEMENT IN INTERNET COMMUNICATION PROJECTS

7.1   Internet Communication Projects

The most popular services provided by the Internet are communication services. These include e-mail, chat rooms, newsgroups, video conferencing, and bulletin boards. This probably does not surprise you. As you may recall, the first idea that led to the construction of the Internet was the U.S. Department of Defense's desire to allow two or more of its military computers to communicate with one another. The next idea that led to the explosive growth of the Internet was the National

Science Foundation making it possible for scientists all over the U.S. to communicate and collaborate on non-military research projects through the NSFNET. Therefore, the Internet is, first and foremost, a communication medium.

The main channels for educators to discharge their educational responsibilities are communication channels: voice, books, videos, radios, TVs, and so on. It is, therefore, natural and appropriate that the communication capabilities of the Internet be applied to educational activities. Internet activities that use these channels often involve collaboration among different, and at time diverse, groups of participants. For this reason, they are often referred to as **collaborative projects.**

The challenge, however, is to determine the most efficient way to use e-mail, chat rooms, video conferencing, bulletin boards, et cetera, to enhance the education process. We must also address the issues that are likely to pop up as a result of using this new communication medium for education.

7.2 How Internet Communication Channels Enhance Education

1. It can be used to collaborate in important projects in any part of the world. One does not need to be physically present to be an active participant in such a project. An individual in the most remote part of the world can communicate with another individual or with an expert in the most advanced parts of the globe through e-mail, video conferencing or Internet Relay Chats. Those who participate in these projects learn about different cultures, teamwork, and respect for others.

2. Many people are excited and motivated to be involved in technological and innovative projects. If properly channeled, this interest could enhance the learning process.

3. Online projects allow participants to be active learners, creators, and owners of their own knowledge, thus preparing them to be independent thinkers and critical evaluators of information.

4. An online learning environment enables educators to be coaches and facilitators of knowledge creation, and not the givers of knowledge.

5. It is real time. It takes only minutes or seconds to communicate via e-mail. Thus, projects that involve collection of current data such as weather forecasts, fluctuations in the stock market, changes in interest rates, et cetera, can benefit from Internet communication in a way never before dreamed of.

6. It addresses some fairness issues. It is color, race, and gender blind. Anyone with access to the Internet, irrespective of economic status, can access the same information as anybody else. Search tools do not recognize social status.

7. Most of the Internet projects involve writing, which is known to enhance critical thinking and concept mastery.

7.3   Types of Collaborative Projects on the Internet

As pointed out at the beginning of this chapter, Internet communication or collaborative projects are those projects that allow the participants to join other participants in other cities or countries in a group activity via e-mail, video conferencing, and so on. The three main types of Internet collaborative projects discussed herein are:

One-to-One Collaborative Projects:

There are projects on the Internet that allow an individual participant to communicate with another participant or an expert about a topic or a special activity of interest. These types of projects are called **one-to-one collaborative projects**. They are easy to set up but difficult to evaluate against achieving educational objectives. For example, it is possible for a one-to-one online project about insects to end with discussions about reptiles if there is no self-restraint by participants or good monitoring by somebody else.

Before getting yourself involved in one of these one-to-one projects, you must establish some evaluation criteria for measuring success that is acceptable to all parties participating in the project. Since the individual participant is the principal investigator in a one-to-one project, some of these projects may not be ideal for unmotivated individuals.

Many-to-One or One-to-Many Collaborative Projects:
In a many-to-one project, a group of individuals can formulate a problem and send it to an expert in the field via e-mail. The expert solves the problem and sends back a solution within a given timeframe. The process continues throughout the duration of the project.

A one-to-many communication project, on the other hand, is the opposite of the many-to-one project. An example of such a project is a video conferencing situation, where an expert addresses a group of participants in different cities and/ or in different countries at the same time. The groups can call or fax questions to the expert during the conference and receive answers instantly or during the session.

Many-to-Many Collaborative Projects
This is the case in which a group of participants collaborates with another group of participants in an online project. The two groups can be from the same geographic region or they can be thousands of miles apart. To start such a project, the different teams form a chat room, a newsgroup or a mailing list. In a problem-solving situation, each participating team can post a challenge problem to the rest of the group to be solved using agreed upon criteria. In another setting, participants from different groups all over the world can collaborate with a group of experts on a subject or topic of interest by means such as video conferencing and e-mail.

7.4 Issues Raised by Internet Collaborative Projects

You must be sure that an online project meets your specific goals before you opt for it. Many individuals or groups get involved in these projects without complete knowledge of what the project is all about, what is expected for successful completion, or how the project adds value to their specific needs. The fact that a friend successfully and enjoyably completed a project does not necessarily mean that it would be a successful and an enjoyable project for you. Below are questions that you have to ask yourself before you commit to joining any online project. These will help you to evaluate different online projects to ensure that your specific needs are met.

Check List for Online Collaborative Projects

1. How do I know that this project is of high quality and meets my specific needs?

2. What kind of evaluation criteria should I use to evaluate this project?
3. How will the project objectives be assessed? How do I measure success?
4. For projects involving students:
   a. How will the students be graded?

b. What about students who don't have access to the Internet from home? Will they be disadvantaged by the project?

c. What steps should be taken to ensure that students are actively involved in the project from day one till the last day?

d. How will this project affect group management?

e. Are my students sufficiently prepared, both intellectually and emotionally, to join in this project? If not, what should I do to bring them up to an appropriate level to ensure success in the project?

f. Will I get the level of support I need to successfully complete the project? This could be both in terms of equipment and moral support. It is essential that the administration, assuming you're working for somebody, be supportive of your efforts in case you run into problems as a result of your getting students involved in the online project.

7.5   Evaluating Internet Collaborative Projects

You have found an Internet collaborative project that looks interesting. How do you know it will satisfy your specific needs? Below are criteria you should use to evaluate the project. To help further in fully understanding the evaluation process, a demonstration on how to evaluate a collaborative project from the Internet is also provided. In the discussions that follow, we shall also assume that you may be getting others involved in these projects.

Evaluation Criteria:
1. Project description and specific requirements
2. Accuracy or reliability of project content
3. Ability to meet education needs
4. Advantage over using traditional materials
5. Equipment and support

Notice that items 2-4 are the same as those for evaluating Internet materials discussed in Chapter 6, and that items 1 and 5 are unique to collaborative projects. Below is a detailed analysis of items 1 and 5:

Project Description and Requirement:
1. What is the project all about?
2. What level of commitment is required in this project?
3. How do I get to participate in the project? How do I get out if I decide not to continue in the project?
4. How will I measure success on this project?

Support and Equipment:
1. What kind of support is provided by the organizers to those who are involved in this project?
2. What kind of equipment is needed to participate in this project?
3. Do my kids or I know how to use the equipment effectively?
4. If the equipment breaks down when the project is on, can I easily fix or replace it?

Evaluation of an Internet Collaborative Project

In June 1998 and 1999, we conducted several Internet workshops for teachers. During the workshop, teachers were asked to evaluate online collaboration projects. Below is one such evaluation:

Evaluator: Eltis Capel, Hamilton County school System, Chattanooga, TN

Web site: http://www.mathforum.org

Title: Ask Dr. nMath

Project description and requirement:

About the project:

Ask Dr. Math is a question and answer service for K-12 math students and their teachers. Dr. Math answers questions about elementary and secondary school mathematics. You can ask questions on homework, puzzles, math contest problems, or any other mathematical topic of interest at the K-12 level. English is the language of communication.

There is also a wealth of information for math professionals about math teaching at the Teacher2Teacher service link. Teachers can also ask questions about teaching by using the math-teach list.

Level of commitment required:

You are expected to check the archives of already answered questions before asking your questions. It is also assumed that you will ask reasonable questions.

Getting to participate or opting out.
A student can join the service by answering a series of simple questions: the student's name, age, e-mail address, and subject of interest. Participation stops when there are no more questions to ask.

Measuring success:
You can measure the success of the project by determining how many questions each of your students asked and by evaluating how the answers helped them solve similar problems. Also look for signs of renewed interest in problem-solving or in mathematics in general.

Figure 7-1. The home page of MathForum that provides a one -to-one collaborative project, Ask Dr. Math.

Accuracy and Reliability:

1. **Author and qualifications**
   Gene Koltz, a professor of mathematics at Swarthmore

College, directs the site. Ask Dr. Math is one of the many services provided at the Mathforum site.

2. **Sponsors**
   The National Science Foundation, Swarthmore College, Microsoft, and Hewlett-Parkard sponsor the projected.

3. **Information reliability**
   Mathematics educators administer the project. Moreover, the sponsors are government, educational, and reputable public corporations. There is an e-mail address for writing the director in case one has a complain or just seeks clarification.

4. **Is the content up to date?** When was it last updated? Activities go on in the site everyday.

5. **Termination date**
   The project is ongoing. You can join any time as described previously.

6. **External site review**
   Ask Dr. Math received an exemplary service award in 1998 and in 1999 from The Virtual Reference Desk Project, a project of the ERIC Clearinghouse on Information & Technology and the U.S. Department of Education's National Library of Education, with support from the White House's Office of Science and Technology Policy.

Ability to Meet Specific Education Needs:

It satisfies education needs since participants ask questions according to their needs. The adult in charge, if kids are involved, should see to it that the kids are asking questions that are relevant to topics discussed by the group.

Advantage Over Traditional Materials

1. **Usage of Internet capabilities.** How would this enhance my lesson?
   Questions are sent to Ask Dr. Math via e-mail. Most of these questions are usually non-textbook types or those with no way of solving using information available from the textbook. The service allows your class to address real-world problems not usually encountered in traditional textbooks. Of course, questions taken from textbooks are also answered.

2. **Quality of related links.**
   There are links to sites that are of interest to math educators and students. The materials on these sites clearly complement the site's materials and goals.

3. **Design of the site**
   The site is easy to navigate. All the links are active. It is easy to get to the home page or other service pages from any of the linked sites. One cannot get lost easily from this site.

Support and Equipment

Any computer with access to the Internet or with an e-mail service can be used to join the project. If you use only an e-mail service, such as Eudora, it must be able to support attachments and graphic files, since answers containing illustrative drawings could be sent through attachment files. Educational support provided at the site includes the following:
   1. The Public Discussion (http://forum.swarthmore. edu/discussions) which lists mathematics and

mathematics education related newsgroups, a
mailing list, and Web-based discussion groups.
2. The Teacher2Teacher (http://forum.swarthmore.
edu/t2t/) site allows the teacher participant to ask
other professionals about mathematics teaching
methods or techniques for learning mathematics.
3. The Forum Web Units and Lessons (http://
forum.swarthmore.edu/web.units.html) site
provides examples of lesson plans that the teacher
can adapt for his/her curriculum needs.

7.6   Resources for Internet Communication Projects.

1.   The MathForum
http://www.mathforum.org
MathForum is an online community of teachers,
students, parents, educators, and citizens who have
an interest in math and math education. Services
provided include a mailing list, Ask Dr. Math, a
discussion group, and a directory of Math Web sites.

2.   Classroom Connect
http://www.classroom.net
This site has many resources and projects for the K-
12 teacher. These projects include GalapagosQuest,
AfricaQuest, and AsiaQuest—now in progress. One
of the unique features of this site is that student
participants can post their work on the site.

3.   NickNacks Telecollaborates
http://www1.minn.net:80/~schubert/
EdHelpers.html#anchor988165

If you want to get your students involved in collaborative projects, then this is a must site to visit. Most of the Internet communication projects are listed here. You would have an opportunity to review many online projects and then choose the best for your class.

4. **Global School House Projects**
http://www.gsn.org/gsn/proj/index.html
This site has a listing of projects sponsored by the Global SchoolHouse. There is also a registry of what they consider the best lessons and projects on the Internet. Moreover, the reader is allowed to create online collaborative projects with site resources.

5. **KidsProj**
http://www.kidlink.org:80/KIDPROJ/
KIDPROJ, which is a project of KIDLINK, allow teachers and youth group leaders from around the world to plan activities and projects for students and other kids age 5 to 15. Current projects include landmark game, I have a dream, and virtual China. In addition to English, projects are done in other languages such as Spanish and Japanese.

6. **Ask-An-Earth-Scientist**
http://www.soest.hawaii.edu/GG/ASK/askanerd.html
This is ask an expert site provided by the Department of Geology and Geophysics, University of Hawaii. You can ask questions about volcanoes, igneous rocks, earthquakes, seismology, natural hazards, geochemistry, the environment, and pollution.

7. **NASA Quest**
http://quest.arc.nasa.gov/interactive/
index.html#archives

NASA Quest projects make it possible for students to meet and interact with NASA scientists, engineers, technicians, and other diverse NASA professionals in online projects. Projects change from time to time. Current projects are Space Team Online, Aero Design Team Online, Women of NASA, and Space Science Online. NASA provides the participant with support not available in many other project sites.

8. **Live From Antarctica2**
   http://quest.arc.nasa.gov/antarctica2/index.html
   This is the site of the award-winning Passport to Knowledge Project. Check this site for oncoming projects.

9. **Amazing Space**
   http://www.stsci.edu/public.html
   The site contains interactive online educational activities from the Hubble Space Telescope.

10. **The Why Files**
    http://news3.news.wisc.edu/cgi-bin/nf/twf/a/1
    The site has a discussion area in which students can participate in science-related discussions.

11. **Virtual Frog Dissection Kit**
    http://www-itg.lbl.gov/vfrog/
    This is the site of the "Whole Frog" project, which allows participants to interactively dissect a frog named Fluffy. Participants can also make movies and play the Virtual Frog Builder Game that is available at the site.

12. **Science Learning Networks**
    http://www.sln.org
    The Science Learning Network has a good collection
    of inquiry-based science projects and lesson plans
    developed by K-12 teachers.

13. **Virtual Field Trip to Antarctica**
    http://www.onlineclass.com/BI/blueice.html
    This site offers a collaborative online field trip to the
    continent of Antarctica. Participants learn about the
    geography, history, and life in the continent. It is an
    on-going project.

14. **Global Grocery List Project**
    http://www.schoollife.net/schools/
    ignore?MIval=cge&GID=
    040020103909221179582226938
    Global Grocery List, which began in 1987, collects
    grocery prices from all over the world. These data
    are used for student computation, analysis, and for
    drawing conclusions in the context of social studies,
    science, mathematics and other disciplines.

15. **I*EARN**
    http://www.igc.apc.org/iearn/
    This is International Education and Resource
    Network. Projects are designed to enable young
    people to contribute meaningfully to the health and
    welfare of the planet and its people. The program is
    truly international, with members from over 60
    countries using over 29 different languages.

16. **Electronic Emissary project**
http://www.tapr.org/emissary/
The Electronic Emissary Project is an online matching service. The program helps K-12 teachers and students locate experts in different disciplines for the purpose of setting up curriculum-based, electronic exchanges.

17. **Good News Bears Stock Market Project**
http://www.ncsa.uiuc.edu:80/edu/RSE/RSEyellow/gnb.html
This is a project specifically designed for middle school students and teachers. In this project, participants do interactive stock market competition using real-time stock market data from the New York Stock Exchange and NASDAQ.

18. **π Mathematics**
http://www.ncsa.uiuc.edu:80/edu/RSE/RSEorange/buttons.html
There is a project that explores the history and applications of the irrational number π on this site. This is a good supplement to a lesson on areas or circumferences.

19. **MegaMath**
http://www.c3.lanl.gov/mega-math
MegaMath is a project of the Computer Research and Applications Group at Los Alamos National Laboratory. It brings important mathematical ideas to k-12 classrooms so that young people and their teachers can think about them together.

20. The MAD Scientist Network
http://www.madsci.org/
This site allows students to ask science questions of the students and faculty of Washington University medical School.

21. Ask a Geologist
http://walrus.wr.usgs.gov/docs/ask-a-ge.html
In this site you can ask questions about geology subjects such as volcanoes, earthquakes, mountains, rocks, maps, ground water, lakes, or rivers.

22. KidsConnect
http://www.ala.org/ICONN/AskKC.html
KidsConnect, sponsored by the American Association of School Librarians, is a question-answering and referral service to K–12 students on the Internet. The goal is to help students access and use information available on the Internet in a responsible way.

23. Ask an Expert Page
http://njnie.dl.stevens-tech.edu/curriculum/aska.html
This site provides information on where to find an expert in many subject areas.

Resource for Finding Partners

1. Keypals
http://www.keypals.com
This is a resource site for finding pen pals.

2. Intercultural E-Mail Classroom Connections
http://www.iecc.org

The IECC (Intercultural E-Mail Classroom Connections) is a free service to help teachers link with partners in other countries and cultures for e-mail classroom pen pal and project exchanges. IECC claims to have distributed over 28,000 requests for e-mail partnerships since its inception in 1992.

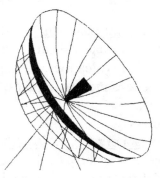

7.7 Resource for Chat Rooms, Discussion Groups, and Listservs

1. Talk City EduCenter
http://www.talkcity.com/educenter
This is an online educational forum. It is designed to facilitate communication among all who share a common interest in the pursuit for quality education. The EduCenter provides online dialogue discussions, workshops, and classroom curriculum projects for members.

2. Teachers.net
http://www.teachers.net
The site provides most, if not all, of the services that a teacher needs for joining a mailing list, discussion group, or chats.

3. **Yahoo's Education Index**
   http://www.yahoo.com/education/
   This is a comprehensive index of educational sites.

4. **Wnetschool**
   http://www.wnet.org/wnetschool/
   In addition to lesson plans and forums, this resource center also provides free workshops to members.

5. **Mailing List Directory**
   http://List-Universe.com/
   This site lists most of the mailing lists on the Internet. In addition, tips and tricks on how to maintain a mailing list are given. If you plan to establish a mailing list for your class, then you should visit this site. See also http://tile.net/lists/.

6. **LISTSERV.HEANET.IE**
   listserv@listserv.hea.ie
   This site gives a comprehensive list of mailing lists on the Internet including numbers of subscribers.

7. **Edupage**
   http://www.educause.edu/pub/edupage/edupage.html
   Edupage is a free e-mail service that summarizes developments in information technology. It is sent three times a week to subscribers. Edupage offers synopses of a more general nature on educational technology, which are extracted from the mainstream media.

8. MathArchives
http://archives.math.utk.edu/archives.html
This is one of the most comprehensive listings of mathematics resources on the Internet. The goal is to provide organized Internet access to a wide variety of mathematical resources with emphasis on materials which are used in the teaching of mathematics.

Part IV

Ethical and Accountability Issues

In Part III you picked Internet materials or communication projects of your choosing after an extensive evaluation. It is being professional to acknowledge the ownership of these Internet materials in your work. If the materials are images or other creative work, you may have to obtain permission before using them. In Chapter 8, we discuss ways of citing different type of Internet materials. Situations where it may be necessary to obtain permission before using Internet materials are discussed in Chapter 9. Online netiquette, which is essential for ethical involvement in collaborative projects, is discussed in Chapter 10. There are many who disagree on the use of the Internet in education. Their views are examined in Chapter 11.

Chapter 8

CITING INTERNET SOURCES

Citing Internet resources is one of the responsible uses of the Internet for research. The reasons for citing the sources of materials we use for research include:

1. Giving credit to those whose work or ideas we have used for our research.
2. Showing that the project we are working on is a part of a bigger body of knowledge.
3. Providing the reader with an opportunity to verify the accuracy of our work.
4. Furnishing the reader with the opportunity to learn more about the area of our research work.

You should cite all sources used for research. It is a good habit, and may at times be unethical, if not criminal, not to do so. Moreover, citing sources would lead to a reduction of plagiarism in research work. A good citation or reference must be complete. A complete reference, whether the document is from a traditional journal or from the Internet, should contain all the information the reader needs to easily identify the document. Thus a citation must contain the name of the author, the title of the cited work, the publisher or the Web site address, and the date of publication or the date the material was accessed.

There are many recommendations on the structure of Internet citations. Right now there is no universally acceptable format. A guiding principle is to follow a format that can be easily understood and which contains all information needed to identify the document. The examples below follow the spirit of the online formats as advocated by Janice R. Walker and Todd Taylor in their book *The Columbia Guide to Online Style*.

The first set is for humanities and is based on the style criteria of the Modern Languages Association of America (MLA). The second set is for scientific writing and is based on the style criteria of the *Publication Manual* of the American Psychological Association (APA). The Alliance for Computers and Writing has endorsed the APA format.

It is important to note that these formats may change over time. Moreover, note that this chapter is not intended to be a complete lesson on citing Internet resources but rather an indication of what is available in this area. For most of you, the sections covered should suffice. For complete treatment of the Columbia Guide and other online style suggestions, see the references at the end of this chapter.

8.1 Online Citation Format for Humanities

8.1.1 Citation Structure for World Wide Web Sites

1. The author of the document, if known: Last Name, First Name.
2. The title of the document: The title should be placed in quotation marks. If a part of a bigger work, the title of the complete work should follow in Italics.
3. Date of creation and file number: Give version or file number, if applicable, and then the date of creation or date of last revision, if available.
4. The Web address-URL: This should include the protocol, the domain name, the directory path, and the file name.

5. The date the document was accessed or downloaded from the Internet: Place this information in parenthesis.

Remarks: The name of the author can be the name of an organization or the maintainer of the site, if no author is listed. If a piece of information is not available, then it cannot be listed. See example 3 below in this section. These remarks apply to all the citation structures below.

Examples:
1. Walker, Janice R. "COS-Humanities Style." *The Columbia Guide to Online Style*. January 1, 1999. http://www.cas.usf.edu/english/walker/ mla.html#1 (June 17, 1999)
2. University of Tennessee at Chattanooga. "Buying Software." June 11, 1999. http:// www.utc.edu/ helpdesk/ (June 17, 1999)
3. "The Arts of Vodoo." http://www.vodoo.org/ arts-syle/style.html (December 12, 1990)

8.1.2 Citation Structure for E-mail, Listserv, and Newsgroups

1. The author of the document, if known: Last Name, First Name or e-mail identification.
2. The subject line of the posting enclosed in quotes.
3. The date the message was sent, if different from the access date.
4. The name of the list or group in italics, if applicable.
5. The full address of the list or group.
6. The date the document was accessed or downloaded from the Internet in parenthesis.

Examples:
1. Aebiefun. "Class Assignment #1." June 5, 1995.
   Teaching Mathematics with the Internet Listserv.
   THEC99 thec99@raven.utc.edu (June 17, 1999).
2. Gideon, Udo. "Re: What is the matter." 02
   February 2000 ugidean@harpo.tnstate.edu (03
   February 2000)
3. Smith, John. "Be my Pal" *Kids Mailing List*
   joinkids@vms.cis.pitt.edu (04 June 1999)

8.1.3 Citation Structure for File Transfer Protocol-FTP
1. The author of the document, if known: Last Name,
   First Name
2. The title of the document in quotes. If a part of a
   larger work, the title of the complete work should
   follow in italics.
3. Document date.
4. The protocol or full ftp address.
5. The date the document was accessed or
   downloaded from the Internet: This information
   should be in parenthesis.

Examples:
1. Diya, Alabi. "HTML for Beginners." 23 July 1985
   ftp://ftp.dlabi.com/pub/alabi/begin.html (05
   October 1991)
2. Bassy, Paul. "Spider Dance Forms." *Dances of
   the Animals.* 12 May 1993.
   ftp://dance.forms.com/pub/pbspider/110593 (09
   December 1998)

8.1.4 Citation Structure for Telnet Sites
1. The author of the document, if known: Last Name,
   First Name or Alias

2. The title of the document, if applicable: The title in quote, the title of the complete work or the telnet site, if applicable, in italics
3. Date of creation or publication, if applicable.
4. The telnet address. This should include the directory path.
5. The date when the site was visited: Place this information in parenthesis.

Examples:
1. Joseph, Beda. "New Age Applications." telnet://rita.nap.org: 997744 Examples (06 March 1997).
2. kostiva (#89899). "Teaching Well." 14 October 1989. *The Arts of Teaching.* telnet://kost.well.com: 5555 good teaching (11 September 1992).

8.1.5 Citation Structure for Talk, Internet Relay Chat, and Multi-User-Dungeon

1. Name or nickname (handle) of speaker: Last Name, First Name.
2. Type of communication: Personal interview, conference, lecture, etc. Conference session title or lecture title in quotes, if applicable.
3. The site title in italics, if applicable.
4. The full address-URL, if applicable: This should include the protocol, the domain name, the directory path, and the file name.
5. The date of communication placed in parenthesis.

Examples:
1. Galico, Tom. Lecture. "The New Copyright Law."
   Ethics in Communication.
   telnet://tom.cecasun.edu: 5555 copy right (10
   October 1982).
2. Baba. Personal Interview. Harpoo. telnet://
   harpoo.uniuyo.edu:8888 (15 July 1991)

8.1.6 Citation Structure for Gopher Sites
1. The author of the document, if known: Last Name,
   First Name.
2. The title of the document in quotes. If a part of a
   bigger work, the title of the complete work should
   follow in italics.
3. Date of publication: Give edition, if applicable
4. The gopher address-URL: This should include the
   protocol, the search or directory path, and the file
   name.
5. The date the document was accessed or
   downloaded from the Internet placed in
   parenthesis, if applicable.

Examples:
1. St. Charles, Grace. " Women Circumcision in
   Africa." 23 February 1987.
   gopher://gopher.unical.edu.nig:87/02/23 africa.wc
   (1 March 1990).
2. UTC Help Desk. "Note for Gopher Beginners."
   Help Desk Gopher Resources.
   gopher://gopher.cecamoon.utc.edu: hd/
   gopherhelp/beginners. (2 June 1994).

8.1.7 Citation Structure for Electronic Publication and Online Databases

1. The author of the article, if known: Last Name, First Name.
2. The title of the article in quotes.
3. The title of the software publication in italics.
4. Date of publication and file number: Give version or edition, and file number, if applicable, and then the date of publication or date of last revision, if available.
5. The name of database service in italics, if applicable.
6. The name of online service in italics, if applicable. Or Internet protocol, the domain name, the directory path, and the file name.
7. The date the publication was accessed or downloaded from the Internet placed in parenthesis. If CD-ROM, accessed date is not applicable.

Examples:

1. Trotter, Andrew. "Training Called Key to Enhancing Use of Computers, Poll Finds." *Education Week*, 16 April 1997. http://edweek.org/ew/vol-16/29jost.h16 (7 December 1999).
2. Todd, Hendric. "Easy Comes Easy Goes." *The New Age*. 19 June 1992 CD-ROM. MORECEC-92 Vol-12 Article 0319.

8.1.8 Citation Structure for Software Programs and Video Games

1. The author of the software, if known: Last Name, First Name.

2. The title of the software program: The title of the software program in italics; give version number, if available.
3. City: Publisher and date of publication, if available.

Examples:
1. Thinkwell. *Demo: Mathematical titles.* Austin: Thinkwell, 2000.
2. Disney/PIXAR. *Toy story 2 CD - RM sampler.* Disney Interactive. 1999

8.2 Online Citation Format for Scientific Writing

8.2.1 Citation Structure for World Wide Web
1. The author of the document, if known: Last Name, Initials, if known.
2. Year of publication in parenthesis.
3. The title of the document: If a part of a bigger work, the title of the complete work follows in italics. In both cases, capitalize only the first word and proper nouns.

4. Give version or file number in parenthesis
5. The Web address-URL: This should include the protocol, the domain name, the directory path, and the file name.
6. The date the document was accessed or downloaded from the Internet placed in parenthesis.

Remarks: The name of the author can be the name of an organization or the maintainer of the site, if no author is listed. If a piece of information is not available, then it cannot be listed. See example 3 below in this section. These remarks apply to all the citation structures below.

Examples:
1. Maurice, C. (1999). Citing electronic information in history papers. http://www.people.memphis.edu/~mcrouse/elcite.html (August 28, 1999).
2. University of Tennessee at Chattanooga. (1999). Buying software. http://www.utc.edu/helpdesk/ (June 17, 1999)
3. The Arts of Vodoo.(1990). http://www.vodoo.org/arts-syle/style.html (December 12, 1992)

8.2.2 Citation Structure for E-mail, Listservs, and Newsgroup
1. The author of the document, if known: Last Name, Initials or e-mail identification.
2. The date he message was sent in parenthesis, if different from accessed date.
3. The subject line of the document: Capitalize only the first word and proper nouns.
4. The name of the list or group in italics, if applicable.

Capitalize only the first word and proper nouns.
5. The name of the group or the protocol and the full address.
6. The date the document was accessed or downloaded from the Internet placed in parenthesis.

Examples:
1. Aebiefun. (1995). Class assignment #1. *Teaching mathematics with the Internet. THEC99.* THEC99 thec99@raven.utc.edu (June 17, 1999).
2. Gideon, U. (2000). Re: What is the matter. ugidean@harpo.tnstate.edu (03 February 2000
3. Smith, J. Be my pal *Kids mailing list* joinkids@vms.cis.pitt.edu (04 June 1999)

8.2.3 Citation Structure for File Transfer Protocol
1. The author of the document, if known: Last Name, Initials, if known.
2. Year of publication in parenthesis.
3. The title of the document: Capitalize only the first word and proper nouns. If a part of a bigger work, the title of the complete work follows in italics. In both cases, capitalize only the first word and proper nouns
4. Give previous publication information, if available.
5. The protocol or full ftp address.
6. The date the document was downloaded from the Internet placed in parenthesis.

Examples:
1. Diya, A.(1985). HTML for beginners. ftp://ftp.dlabi.com/pub/alabi/begin.html (05 October 1991)

2. Bassy, P. (1993). Spider dance forms. *Dances of the animals* ftp://dance.forms.com/pub/pbspider/110593 (09 December 1998)

8.2.4 Citation Structure for Telnet Sites

1. The author of the document: Last Name, Initials, and alias, if known.
2. Date of publication in parenthesis.
3. The title of the document: The title of the complete work or Telnet site follows in italics. Capitalize only the first word and proper nouns
4. The full telnet address. This should include port number and command sequence, if applicable, and the directory path.
5. The date when the site was visited placed in parenthesis.

Examples:

1. Joseph, B. D. (1992) New age applications. telnet://rita.nap.org: 997744 Examples (06 March 1997).
2. kostiva (#89899). Teaching Well. *The arts of teaching.* telnet://kost.well.com: 5555 good teaching (11 September 1989).

8.2.5 Citation Structure for Talk, Internet Relay Chat, Multi-User-Dungeon

1. Name or nickname (handle) of speaker: Last Name, initials
2. Type of communication: Personal interview, conference, lecture, etc.

Give conference session title or lecture title, if applicable.
3 The site title in italics, if applicable.
4. The full URL address.
5. The date of communication placed in parenthesis.

Examples:
1. Galico, T. Lecture. The new copyright law. *Ethics in communication.* telnet://tom.cecasun.edu: 5555 copy right (10 October 1982).
2. Baba. Personal interview. Harpoo. telnet://harpoo.uniuyo.edu:8888 (15 July 1991)

8.2.6 Citation Structure for Gopher Sites
1. The author of the document, if known: Last name, initials, if known.
2. Date of publication in parenthesis.
3. The title of the document: If a part of a bigger work, the title of the complete work or gopher site follows in italics, if applicable. In all cases, capitalize only the first word and proper nouns.
4. The gopher address-URL: This should include the protocol, the search path or directory path, and the file name.
5. The date the document was accessed or downloaded from the Internet placed in parenthesis.

Examples:
1. St. Charles, G. (1987). Women circumcision in Africa.
   gopher://gopher.unical.edu.nig:87/02/23 africa.wc

(1 March 1990).
2. UTC Help Desk. Note for gopher beginners. *Help desk gopher resources.* gopher://gopher.cecamoon.utc.edu:hd/gopherhelp/ beginners. (2 June 1994).

8.2.7 Citation Structure for Electronic Publication and Online Databases
1. The author of the document, if known: Last name, initials, if known.
2. Date of publication in parenthesis.
3. The title of the document: Capitalize only first word and proper nouns.
4. The title of the database in italics; the name of the online service in italics.
5. The full online address of publisher or database service. This should include the protocol, the domain name, the directory path, and the file name.
6. The date the publication was accessed or downloaded from the Internet placed in parenthesis. If CD-ROM, accessed date is not applicable.

Examples:
1. Trotter, A. (1997). Training called key to enhancing use of computers, poll finds. *Education Week.* http://edweek.org/ew/vol-16/29jost.h16 (7 December 1999).
2. Todd, H. (1992). Easy comes easy goes. *The new age.* CD-ROM. MORECEC-92 Vol-12 Article 0319.

8.2.8 Citation Structure for Software Programs and Video Games

1. The author of the document, if known: Last name, initials, if known.
2. Date of publication in parenthesis.
3. The title of the software program in italics. Capitalized only first word and proper nouns. Give a version number, if applicable.
4. City: publisher.

Examples:

1. Thinkwell (2000). *Demo CD: Mathematical titles.* Austin: Thinkwell.
2. Disney/PIXAR. (1999). *Toy story 2 CD - RM sampler.* Disney Interative.

References

1. Classroom Connect. How to Cite Internet Resources. http://classroom.com/resource/CitingNetResources.asp (September 1999)
2. Connected Teacher. Citing Internet Sources. http://connectedteacher.com/newsletter/citeintres.asp (February, 2000)
3. Crouse, M. (1999). Citing electronic information in history papers. http://www.people.memphis.edu/~mcrouse/elcite.html (August 28, 1999)
4. Journalism Resources. Karla's Guide to Citation Guides. http://bailiwick.lib.uiowa.edu/journalism/cite.html (September 1999).
5. Li and Crane (1996). Electronic Styles: A handbook for Citing Electronic Information.

Information Today, Inc., New Jersey.
6. PBS Adult Learning Satellite Services (2002). Evaluating Resources for Learning Online. Live via Satellite, 2:00-3:30 pm, April 12, 2002.
7. UT Chattanooga Library's Guide for Style Manuals. Locating Style Manuals. http://www.lib.utc.edu/library/handouts/other/webeval42.doc (April 15, 2002)
8. Walker, J. (1996). APA-Style Citation of Electronic Sources. http://www.columbia.edu/cu/cup/cgos/idx_basic.ht (July 10, 1999).
9. Walker, J. and Taylor, T. (1998). The Columbia Guide to Online Style. Columbia University Press, New York.
10. Widener University and Wolfgram Memorial Library. Evaluating Web Pages: Links to various concepts. http://www.science.widener.edu/~withers/examples.htm

Chapter 9

Online Netiquette:
How to Behave in Cyberspace

Netiquette, an acronym of InteNet and ETIQUETTE, is the set of rules that govern proper behavior of members of the Internet community. It is not different from the standard polite behavior expected from members of any civilized community. As there is no Internet police force, at least for now, it is incumbent on every person using the Internet to keep it civilized so that governments are not forced to regulate this global community.

You heard it is right! The Internet is a global community. It is bigger than a single country or continent. This very nature of the Internet community complicates the netiquette issue. This is because some words, phrases or expressions do have slightly different meanings in different parts of the globe due in part to local cultural differences among nations. For example, an expression that might be okay for an American might be insulting to a Japanese or an African. In using the communication channels of the Internet, one needs to be mindful of these differences in word usage.

What is a proper behavior in a divergent community? In my opinion, the rule of thumb should be the Golden

Rule: *Do onto others what you would have them do onto you.* Although not a hundred percent sufficient, it is certainly a good starting point. Below are specific ways to be civilized when using the different communication channels of the Internet.

9.1 E-mail Netiquette

1. Language

Be mindful of your language at all times. The tone of your e-mail tells your mood at the time of writing and may reflect your character. Writing when angry or using mean, insulting, and sarcastic words or expressions in your e-mail message reflects negatively on you. On the other hand, showing politeness and good demeanor in your message puts you in a positive opinion of the recipient. Remember that an unknown receiver of your message could be your dad, a future spouse or employer! You don't want to make a mistake now and regret later, especially when it is an avoidable one.

In addition to being mindful of your words, you should also be careful about the quality of your writing. Since your e-mail message may be used to judge your character and communication abilities, taking time to compose your message is worth the effort. Avoid grammatical errors, if possible. The best way to minimize grammatical errors is to use a word processing software, such as Microsoft Word or WordPerfect.

The level of education of users of the Internet differs, and for some, English is not their first language. Consequently, you must be concise, straight to the point, and avoid using big sounding vocabularies in all Internet communications. Avoid using slang, as well as some humor, as their meanings may be misunderstood by those not from your geographical area. Also, do not use capital letters when sending e-mail. In the Internet community, using all capitals to type your message means you are shouting at the receiver. If you want to emphasize a point, you may consider using "quotes" or *italics*.

2. Length of an E-mail Message

An e-mail message should be short and straight to the point. Many people are impatient reading long e-mails. In addition, long e-mails take storage space that your recipient may not have. If the recipient is using a free e-mail account, then he or she is limited on the length of the messages he or she can get through the server. Thus a lengthy e-mail will not be delivered to the intended recipient in this circumstance.

One way to avoid a lengthy e-mail is to use an attachment. However, it is advisable to find out if the receiver accepts attachments. Verifying acceptance of attachment is important because the receiver's e-mail software may not be able to handle attachments or there is no space for large files in the receiver's computer. For example, if the file is too large, it may prevent the receiver's computer from accepting other mails. This is not fair to the recipient.

Delete the header when replying to an e-mail message. It could make the message unreasonably long, but without offering any useful information to the recipient. It is also not necessary to attach the original message with your reply. You can delete some portion of the original message and retain only those lines that relate to your reply. The author had a bad experience forwarding an interesting message to a mailing list. I did not delete the header, which was long by any standard, since the message had passed through many hands before getting to me. I was very surprised at how many people got mad at me, and many of them were nice people. The message I wanted to pass along got submerged in the process. Nobody seemed to have noticed the message, but only the long header. Do not allow this to happen to you.

3. The E-mail Subject Line
The subject line describes the content of the e-mail message. When you open an e-mail message using most e-mail clients, such as Eudora, you see two to five columns. In any e-mail client you use, there must be a column (or a header) that gives you the identification or e-mail address of the sender, a column for date, and a column for the subject line. If the sender gives no subject line, then most programs may insert the phrase "no subject" in the place of the actual subject line.

You should always use an appropriate subject line to describe the content of your message. Many recipients may delete, without reading, an e-mail with no subject line. To some recipients, this is an insulting act, while some may think that you are hiding something ominous, especially if they don't know you.

Finally, make the subject line brief and concise, about 15-25 characters. It should be a good summary of your e-mail message.

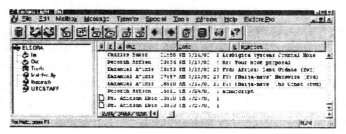

4. The Signature File

A signature file allows you to attach personal information at the end of an e-mail message, so that you don't have to retype the information during each e-mail session. A signature file should be brief, not more than about six lines. Information you may consider including in your signature file:

Name; title and rank, if appropriate
· Place of work
Work address
Work phone numbers, including extension, if appropriate
Internet address, if available
Character quote, optional

The author has seen people include their home phone numbers in the signature file. Please think twice before you do this. It is also not necessary to include your e-mail address since it's already in the header. Of course, you can include other e-mail addresses in the signature file.

If your children use e-mail, then you must be careful allowing them to use signature files. If in a school environment, it is advisable not to allow students to use signature files when using the school e-mail account. If a student has a private e-mail account, then require the student to seek the permission of a parent or a guardian before making a signature file.

5. Formatting

The Internet is platform independent. This makes it possible to use different computers and different software brands to send e-mail to be received by somebody using a different computer or software. Although you may use Eudora to send mail to be received by someone using Pine, the two e-mail clients may decode messages differently. Thus if you spend time to format your message, there is no reason to believe that the recipient will receive the message with the format intact. Apart from wasting time, your formatted message may become a bunch of meaningless characters on the screen of the recipient if his or her e-mail client has no capability to properly decode your formatted message. You should use plain text with no color, bold face or HTML tags when sending an e-mail message, unless you are sure that the recipient's e-mail client can properly decode your formatted message.

6. Images and Bandwidth

Pictures and other images require an enormous storage space. If the recipient's bandwidth is small, and so cannot accommodate the size of your image, it may be seen on the screen as a bunch of good for nothing special characters. The recipient will not be able to make any sense from them. Even when there is enough space to store the image in the hard drive, the size of the image may prevent the recipient from receiving more e-mail messages or being able to save a computer file to the hard drive. If you are sending a large image file, netiquette demands that you notify the recipient and get permission before e-mailing your image file.

7. Attending to Mail

Read your mail regularly or transfer it from the server to your computer. Do not store your mail on the server for too long, as it consumes bandwidth. To avoid one person taking up too much bandwidth, many e-mail server managers delete messages after about two weeks. You may want to find out from your server manager what is the policy in your situation.

Although you should read your mail regularly, you must avoid the temptation of clicking on the mail client every second. It is time wasting and could lead to low productivity. Many organizations are now concerned about the amount of time their employees are spending sending, receiving, or surfing the Internet. It is difficult to have an optimum number of times to check for e-mail. It will depend on individuals and circumstances. But reading your mails about three times a day, morning, afternoon, and evening is good starting point. After some time, you can adjust this rate to suit your special circumstances.

If you are traveling out of town, you can inform the server manager so that he/she doesn't delete your messages. Some e-mail programs, such as Eudora, allow you to automatically delete a message from the server after a certain number of days using the option menu in the tool bar as shown in the diagram below. In addition, the message can be automatically transferred to your computer each time you check your e-mail by checking the box that says "send on check" and leaving blank the box that says "leave mail on the server".

An e-mail lies between a phone conversation and a formal letter. Many people who send out e-mail messages expect the receiver to reply to their mail promptly. It is good netiquette to reply to your mail promptly. If for good reason you cannot do so, an acknowledgement of receipt of the e-mail is encouraged.

Finally, if your e-mail message has an attachment, you should be careful opening it. An attachment that contains a computer virus can destroy the content of your computer. The rule of thumb is not to open any attachment that you do not expect, even from a person you know. Virus programs can send themselves, using a stolen computer address of someone you know. If in doubt, delete it or call the sender to confirm.

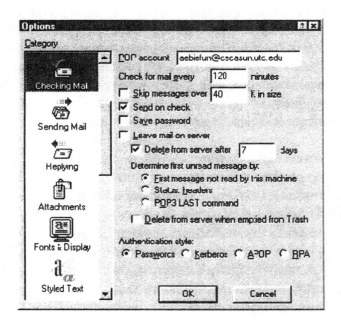

8. The Flaming Act

This is the practice of posting offensive, annoying, objectionable, hateful, and what have you, messages. Please do not send or reply to flame messages. My experience is that most of the messages perceived as offensive are not really offensive after a careful reading or they are totally misunderstood. It may be a joke, a humor or a slang you don't understand. Suppose, in the worse case, that somebody is insulting you through e-mail. You show greater wisdom by not flaming back.

Nevertheless, any information that is a misrepresentation of facts and which is damaging should be corrected. Even in this exceptional situation, you can still reply to the e-mail without flaming back.

9. Chain Letters

Have you ever received a letter that is chained up or wrapped in chains? You probably have not. The post office may not accept such letters. However, by a chain letter, we mean a letter that is sent from one person to another in a repeated fashion. Most of the time, these letters give alert to a computer virus or tell a story that sounds too good to be true, which forces the uncanny to pass it along to good friends.

Chain letters are not common with snail mail, such as from the post office, because of the cost involved. They are common with e-mail since it is easy to use the forward feature of an e-mail client to circulate a letter through a mailing list with basically no cost involved.

Please do not send or forward a chain letter. But how do we know that this letter, with potentially useful information, is a hoax? You may check to see if it is listed at the following sites:

http://www.urbanlegends.com/ulz/emailtax.html
http://www.urbanlegends.com/ulz
http://spcup.org/hoax.htm
http://www.sysmantec.com/avcenter/hoax.html
http://urbanlegends.miningco.com
http://antivirus.miningco.com/library/blenhoax.htm

On these sites are listed most of the old and well-known chain letters. If not on any of these sites, you have to make a judgment call. (Note: sites may change over time.)

Suppose you just received a chain letter. What do you do about it? The first instinct in many people is to send the offender an obnoxious e-mail message calling him or her names, and letting him or her know how stupid it is to forward a chain letter. My good friend, this is wrong. Think about it! Why do many people forward a chain letter? From my personal experience, the majority of those who forward chain letters do so believing that they are providing you with useful information, which, unfortunately, turns out to be a hoax. We need to be educative and understanding in our reaction to our friends who forward chain letters to us.

A personal story! I have forwarded chain letters to a mailing list before, with good intentions, only to be told they are hoaxes. (Believe it or not, it is shameful to be told, even politely, that the mail you forwarded is a hoax. It is even worse when it is accompanied by name-calling.) Because of the over-reactive and insulting attitude of some group members, I decided not to forward any information to the group anymore, in case I make a mistake and forward a chain letter. When the Love Bug hit, I got the news many hours before many people in the United States, since I subscribe to an international mailing list where members spread over many time zones, some twelve hours before the United States. However, I did not forward it to the list, in case it was a hoax, but I unplugged my T1 connection for personal protection. Six hours after I read the mail, the story of Love Bug was on the NPR news. Fortunately, our mailing list was not affected by Love Bug. Is there a lesson to be learned from this? I think so. My view is that a person who sends a virus hoax to a list, with good intentions, could one day save the list from a real killer virus. Let us not crucify such an individual.

10. Privacy

There are no privacy guarantees in e-mail. If you are using an organization mail server, then the organization has a legal right to read your e-mail. Even if not read by your boss, your e-mail messages can be easily intercepted somewhere before it gets to its final destination or the recipient can forward it to someone else. To minimize interception of your messages, you may consider using an encryption program such as PGP. However, you have to understand that no encryption program can be one hundred percent foolproof.

If you are using your personal computer, you can use system password or screen saver password to ensure that people don't get in and read your mail when you step out of the office. Remember to delete your mail regular. If you need to keep a mail, you can print it or copy it into your hard drive, and then delete it from your mail folder. Again, note that deleting the mail is not foolproof. It is possible to retrieve a computer file after it has been deleted. Thus, in general, you should assume that an e-mail is, to some extent, a public domain document. The usual advice is not to send by e-mail what you don't want a third person to read.

9.2   Mailing List and Chat Netiquette

Mailing list and Chat room netiquette is not different from that of e-mail. In addition to observing e-mail netiquette, the following netiquette is also recommended for mailing list and chat room environments.

1. When you join a mailing list, do not rush into sending or replying to messages. It is wise to spend some time reading the frequently asked questions (FAQ) page, if available, and the messages and replies from other list members. This will give you a feel of what the group norms are, if not explicitly stated. This is called **lurking**. When you finally start sending or replying to messages, called **d-lurking**, follow the written (or otherwise) norms of the group.

2. It is not necessary to send an answer to a question or a comment to all on a list-serv unless it is of interest to everybody on the list. If somebody had a typo, for example, it is better to inform the person directly rather than through the list.

3. Do not send an announcement to the list if the topic is not of interest to all members. If you are not sure what to do, ask the list administrator for help.

4. Do not send an advertisement to a list server. This is called **spamming**.

5. As a responsible member of a list, do not give the list address to non-members without the knowledge of the list maintainer. Some non-members who have access to the list address are likely to violate the list code of behavior.

6. Newsgroup discussions can be very technical at times. You can strengthen your argument by citing the sources of your facts. In making arguments, be careful not to repeat what has already been said, as this is a waste of the group's time.

7. Newsgroup is a good place to seek advice or information. If you happen to do so, share with

the group a summary of the useful ones you received. By so doing, you not only enrich the knowledge of group members but also prevent somebody asking the same question again later on.

8. Most newsgroups archive the information posted by members. Therefore, your message could be accessed many years later. As in the case of e-mail, assume that anybody can access your message to the group and be mindful of your language.

9.3   Resources for Netiquette Issues

1. The Net: User Guidelines and Netiquette - Index
   http://www.fau.edu/netiquette/net/
2. The Netiquette Homepage by Arlene Rinaldi.
   http://www.fau.edu/netiquette/net/netiquette.html
3. CORE RULES OF NETIQUETTE
   http://www.albion.com/netiquette/corerules.html
4. Netiquette:http://www.in.on.ca/tutorial/
   netiquette.html
5. Business Netiquette International
   http://www.bspage.com/1netiq/Netiq.html
6. Dark   Mountain's   Netiquette   Guide.
   www.darkmountain.com
7. Useful tips by Chuq Von Rospach and Gene Spafford
   http://redtail.unm.edu/cp/netiquette.html
8. Netiquette Guidelines
   http://www.allsands.com/Computers/
   netiquettenethi_hb_gn.htm

9. PBS Beginners Guide to the Internet.
   http://www.pbs.org/uti/guide/netiquette.html
10. A Netiquette Primer http://www.ncte.org/
    resources/primer.html
11. Online Netiquette uncensored. http://
    www.onlinenetiquette.com/
12. Cyber Pet Netiquette: http://www.bearjests.com/
    cyberpet/netiquette.html
13. Tips on Netiquette
    http://www.imaginarylandscape.com/helpweb/
    mail/polite.html
14. Disney Cyber Netiquette Page. http://
    disney.go.com:80/cybersafety/
15. Netiquette Guidelines Center. http://
    www.albury.net.au/new-users/netiquet.htm
16. Netiquette for New User. http://www.ccim.com/
    netiq.htm
17. Patrick Crispens' Road Map 96: Map 07-
    Netiquette. http://netsquirrel.com/roadmap96/
    map07.html
18. An Argument for Netiquette Holds up in Court:
    http://www.nytimes.com/library/tech/99/07/cyber/
    cyberlaw/16law.html
19. The Michigan Electronic Library Internet
    Etiquette.
    http://mel.lib.mi.us/internet/INET-netiquette.html

Chapter 10

Copyright and Fair Use

The essentials of the copyright laws relevant to educators are given in this chapter. The copyright law is vague and complicated and is not covered in detail in this book. For further reading on this topic, refer to the references section at the end of the chapter. You can also obtain useful information on copyright by using the search function of your Web browser.

10.1 Essence of the Copyright Law

Copyright laws protect original works of authors, and other creators, from unauthorized use or copying. The copyright holder, which may or may not be the author, has the *exclusive right* to reproduce, distribute, make derivative work, and publicly perform or display the work. The provision applies to both published and unpublished works in areas that include:
1. Literary works including computer programs,
2. Musical and dramatic works,
3. Pictorial, graphical, and other artistic works,
4. Motion pictures and other audio visual works,
5. Sound recording,
6. Architectural works, and
7. Pantomimes and choreographic works.

The authorship could be by a single individual, a group of individuals, or by an organization.

10.2   Fair Use of Copyrighted Materials

The Copyright Law has a fair use provision. This provision allows a limited reproduction of copyrighted works, without permission from the copyright holder, for educational purposes such as teaching, research, and criticism.

As an educator, how do you know that the picture, web page, or the portion of a book you downloaded from the Internet to be included in your class website meets the fair use criteria? To answer this question correctly, you must evaluate your actions against the following criteria listed in the law:

1.   The *purpose* and *character* of the use
    Purpose: Is it for educational use? If so, is it for teaching, research, or criticism?
    Are you going to make money from it?
    Character: Assuming that the purpose of the use is educational, are you going to make handouts from it? Are you going to place it on reserve in the library? Are you going to ask a copy center to make course packs and sell to students? Are you going to benefit financially from the use of the material?
2.   The *nature* of the copyrighted work
    If the work is a public domain document, or does not involve any creativity to produce, then it may be all right to copy and use it. Similarly, you may not get into trouble if the work is out of print, outdated, or the term of the copyright has expired. On the other hand, if the work is

for profit or if the creator does not give up his or her right, it may be illegal to copy and use it without permission.

3. The *amount* and *substantiality* of the portion used in relation to the whole work

    Amount: What percentage of the work are you using? It is correct to assume, in many cases, that the more the quantity use in relation to the whole work, the more likely that it is not a fair use.

    Substantiality: It is possible that the popularity of a creative work depends on a small portion of the work. For example, many of us buy a music CD-ROM because of only one track in the collection. If the quantity you use takes the soul out of the work, then it may not be a fair use, no matter how small the percentage used in relation to the whole work.

4. The marketability of the work

    Who are the potential buyers of the work? If the work is for your students and you copy it for them, then that affects the marketability of the work and may not be a fair use. However, if the work is for bird watchers, and you make few copies for your kids, who are not bird watchers, you may not violate the fair use provision.

In any litigation, you should expect that all the above guidelines would be used to determine liability. But experts and non-experts agree that any use that affects the market value of the work, no matter how small in proportion to the whole work, will carry more weight in determining if your use was a fair use.

10.3 What is not Copyrighted

There are many categories of works that are not protected by the copyright law. These include:

1. Facts, ideas, systems, procedures, methods, processes, and discoveries. However, the ways in which these items are packaged, presented, explained or illustrated may be copyright protected.
2. Works from public domain sources or works consisting entirely of information from a source with no original authorship. Examples of such works include standard calendars, different measurement charts, and some works that are sponsored entirely by the government.
3. Proverb, slogans, names, titles, common symbols or signs and their variations.
4. Works that are not fixed in a tangible form. Examples of such works are choreographic works, speeches, and performances that are not written down, recorded or notated.

10.4 Examples of Fair-use Court Cases

Many fair-use cases have gone to the courts. A careful look at some of these court cases sheds light on the issue of fair-use, especially on course packets.

Basic Books, Inc. v. Kinko's Graphic Corp. (1991): Basic Books sued Kinko's in 1991 for using its publications to make course packs without permission. The court found Kinko's in violation of fair use using the following reasoning:

1. **Purpose**: Kinko's copying was commercial and not educational as Kinko's made profit from it. It was not transformative as Kinko's did not add anything new to the work.
2. **Nature**: Factual works are more amenable to fair use. Kinko's copying was from factual work such as history and economics.
3. **Amount and Substantiality**: The court found that Kinko's copied 5 to 25 percent of each work and that such was excessive. The court also found that the portions copied took the soul out of the work since they were copied because of their importance.
4. **Marketability**: The court found that Kinko's copying undermined the marketability of the books, since the students were buying the course packs and not the books.

Remark:

Kinko's was found guilty because it violated three out of the four fair use criteria. That is, the court will consider the four criteria in determining any fair use case. The court refused the publishers request to ban all anthologies or collected works. The opinion of the court was that collected works must be analyzed on a case by case basis for fair use.

Princeton University Press v. Michigan Document Services (MDS) (1996): In 1996 Princeton University Press sued MDS for making course packs from its books without permission. The case, which was finally settled by all 13 members of the Sixth Circuit Court, found MDS guilty of fair use violation. The 10 judges who voted against MDS reached their decision using the following reasoning:

1. **Purpose:** MDS copying was commercial and not transformative;
2. **Nature:** Some works contained creative material. Works that are "creative" in nature are less susceptible to fair use than factual works.
3. **Amount and Substantiality:** The professors wanted the excerpts because they were very important parts of the entire work. Copies were of high qualitative value.
4. **Marketability:** The loss of permission fees affects the markets for the books.

10.5   Fair Use Guidelines for Classroom Use

The fair use provision in the law is vague. Congress made it that way so that fair use is decided on a case-by-case basis, and not by a precise set of rules that apply to all cases, irrespective of their special circumstances. The confusion caused by the vagueness of the law led a group of educators and publishers to come up with more specific guidelines for fair use, called *Fair Use Guidelines for Classroom Use*, which are listed below. These guidelines should not be taken as the law but as information on the minimum amount of copying that may be done under fair use. There are some groups, such as The American Association of University Professors and The American Association of Law Schools, who oppose the guidelines. These groups believe that the guidelines may lead to more confusion and that some people and the courts may take the guidelines as the law.

1. **Making Single Copies for Research or Teaching**
   a. a book chapter
   b. a periodical or newspaper article
   c. short story, essay, or poem
   d. a picture, chart, graph, diagram, drawing, cartoon and the like from a newspaper, book, or periodical

2. **Making Multiple Copies for Research or Teaching**
   a. Each student may not get more than a copy
   b. Copies made must not be too long. For example, at most 250 words for poems and 2500 words for essays or short stories.
   c. Need is Spontaneous. For example, the copying is done at a time when you must use the work immediately and it is not feasible to ask for permission
   d. Cumulative Effect is Little. For example, you copy for one course rather than multiple courses. Access to the material should be limited.
   e. Copying in order to make, replace, or substitute for anthologies, compilations or collective works is *not* allowed.
   f. Copying consumable works such as workbooks is *not* allowed.
   g. Repeat copying of the same work by the same teacher from time to time is *not* permitted.
   h. Making profit from the copying is *not* permitted. For example, students can only be charged the actual cost of copying of the work.
   i. You may not make multiple copies of a work for classroom use.

In addition to the limits listed above, the "Guidelines" offer rules for copying music and off-air videotaping. The book, "Copyright in the age of new technology" by Bottersbush (1996) discusses the guidelines and fair use for various media, including videotaping of cable and satellite programming.

3. Making Course Packets for Teaching

Although the courts do not ban making of course packs, using the cases against Kinko's and MDS as a guideline, you may not make course packs without permission from the copyright holder.

10.6 Obtaining Permission

The best way to avoid copyright problems is to obtain permission from the copyright owner or the owner's authorized agent. You can do this by either contacting the copyright owner (or agent) directly or by contacting the Copyright Clearance Center (CCC). Information on how to contact the copyright owner is often provided in the work. If this information is not provided, your best bet is to contact the CCC at Copyright Clearance Center, Inc., 222 Rosewood Drive, Danvers, MA 01923 USA. (Phone 978-750-8400, Fax 978-750-4470, E-mail: http:// www.copyright.com/)

In your contact letter, you should include:

1. A return address, E-mail address, fax, and phone numbers.
2. An identification of who you are (including titles) and your institution.

3. A description of how you want to use the material.
4. A complete description of the material you need and where you found it.
5. A description of how the work in which the material is included will be distributed.
6. A space in the letter so that the copyright owner could add comments or conditions.
7. Two copies of the request letter. The copyright owner should sign both letters, keep one, and return one to you in a self-stamped addressed return envelope.
8. A phrase which says that the signing and returning of the letter to you means the signer is the copyright owner and that by signing has given you permission to use the material as you described in your letter.

Sample Form Letter Requesting Permission to Use Copyrighted material.

Dear [*Title and Name*],

I am [*title and job description*] at [*place and address of your work*]. I would like permission to [*describe your intended use of the work*] which is found [*give complete reference to the original work*]. The resulting material will be [*describe how you want to use the work or distribute the resulting work*].

Please let me know your approval of this permission by signing and returning one of the enclosed permission letters at your earliest convenience in the enclosed self-addressed stamped envelope, and keeping one for your records. Please use the space below for your comments, if any.

Thanks.

Your Sincerely,
[*Name, Title*]
Comments:_____

_____

_____

_____

_____

_____

_____

Signature and date:_____

_____

**I am the copyright holder and permission is granted:
signature/date: _____**

10.7 Resources for Copyright and Fair Use

Books/Periodicals

1. Bottersbush, H. R. (1996). Copyright in the age of new technology. Phi Delta Kappa Educational Foundation, Bloomington, Indiana.
2. Bunnin, B. (1990, April). Copyrights & wrongs. Publish, 77-82.
3. Copyright Information Services (1985). The official fair-use guidelines: Complete texts of four official documents arranged for use by educators.

P. O. Box 1460, Friday Harbor, Washington.

4. Copyright Information Kit, United States Copyright Office, Library of Congress, Washington, DC 20559.

5. Crews, K. D. (1995). Copyright law and information policy planning: Public rights of use in the 1990's and beyond. Journal of Government Information, 22 (2), 87-99.

6. Crews, Kenneth D. (1995). Copyright, Fair Use, and the Challenge for Universities: Promoting the Progress of Higher Education. The University of Chicago Press, Chicago, IL.

7. Crews, K. D. (1996). What qualifies as 'fair use'? The Chronicle of Higher Education, 42 (36), B1-B2.

8. Gasaway, L. N. (1995). White paper — a mixed bag. Techtrends, 40 (6), 6-8.

9. Goodell, J. (1988). Copyright law. National Association of Desktop Publishers Journal, 2(1), 147-153.

10. Jacobson, R. L. (1996). The furor over 'fair use.' The Chronicle of Higher Education, 42 (35), A25, A30, A34.

11. Kasunic, R. (1993) Fair use and the educator's right to photocopy copyrighted material for classroom use, Journal of College and University Law, 19(3) 271-293.

12. Kaufman, B. L. (1996). College copy pack ruled infringement. (1996, November 9). Cincinnati (Ohio) Enquirer (Newsbank: EDU 88:F13).

13. Lemmon, B. (February 1992). Copyright in the digital age. Industrial Photography, 20-23.

14. Salpeter, Judy. (June 1992). Are you obeying copyright law? Technology and Learning, 14-23.

Schockmel, R. B. (1996). The premise of copyright, assaults on fair use, and royalty fees. The Journal of Academic Librarianship, 22 (1), 15-25.

15. Speere, L., & Parsons, P. (1995). The copyright implications of using video in the classroom. Journalism and Mass Communication Educator, 49 (4), 11-20.

16. Stansbury, R. (1996) Copyright and distance learning: A balancing act. In E. R. Sinofsky, (Ed.), Copyright and you. Techtrends, 41 (6), 9-11.

17. Zenor, S. D. (1996) Copyright and the internet. Techtrends, 41 (4), 2.

18. Talab, R. S. (1997). An educational checklist for copyright and multimedia. In E.

Online Resources Web Sites

1. Copyright Clearance Center Online. http://www.copyright.com/

2. Crews, K. D. (June 18, 1996). Update on the MDS decision in *Copyright and Intellectual Property* http://arl.cni.org/scomm/copyright/mds.crews.html

3. CSU-SUNY-CUNY Joint Committee on Copyrights and Fair Use (1996). Fair Use of Copyrighted Works: A Crucial Element in Educating America. http://www.cetus.org/fairindex.html (January 5, 2002)

4. White House Information Infrastructure Task Force Working Group (1995). Intellectual Property and the National Information Infrastructure http://www.uspto.gov/web/offices/com/doc/ipnii/ (January 5, 2002)

5. United States Courts of Appeal for the Sixth Circuit (1996). Princeton University Press, MacMillan, Inc., and St. Martin's Press, Inc., v. Michigan Document Services, Inc., and James M. Smith. *ELECTRONIC CITATION: 1996 FED App. 0357P (6th Cir.)* File Name: 96a0357p.06 No. 94-1778 http://fairuse.stanford.edu/mds/110896cofadec.html (December 21, 2001)

6. Rothman, D. H. (1996). Schools, political debate, privacy would suffer under white house's radical proposal on intellectual property, say 100+law professors. http://www.clark.net/pub/rothman/boyle.htm (December 21, 2001)

7. Templeton, B. 10 Big Myths about Copyright Explained. http://www.templetons.com/brad/copymyths.html (December 21, 2001)

8. Stanford University Libraries. Copyright and Fair Use. http://fairuse.stanford.edu/ (January 5, 2002).

9. The Library of Congress (2001). United States Copyright Office. http://lcweb.loc.gov/copyright/ (January 5, 2002)

Chapter 11

Accountability Issues Over Using Technology in the Classroom

The use of the Internet, or technology in general, in the classroom is expensive. In addition to buying hardware and software, the institution or school system must also think about training and reward for faculty members, provision of technical staff, copyright and fair use problems, and student or staff compliance with acceptable use policies. Since money is limited, it may not be possible to fully implement technology in the classroom without letting other programs, such as arts, physical education, and music, go or be under-funded. This situation has led many to ask if the benefit of using technology in the classroom is sufficient to move money away from other areas with proven benefits.

As you probably expected, there is divided opinion on the benefits of computer usage in the classroom, including the Internet. Following are the views of the two camps:

11.1 Supporters' Views
1. There are places where computers are making a difference in the classroom. These exemplary

programs can be adapted with success to the benefit of most students.

2. Most of the studies that show computers are not making a difference are flawed in design.
Well-designed research shows that if computers are properly used, student performance levels are equal to or greater than those of students in the traditional classrooms.

4. It is not the computer by itself but how it is used that makes the difference. They emphasize teacher training as a key to effective use of computer technology in the classroom.

11.2 Non-Supporters' Views

1. The nature of teaching involves human process that cannot be automated as in manufacturing. The human 'touch' is very important in learning and computers cannot replace that. They assert that this needed human touch is lacking when computers replace teachers.

2. There is no hard evidence that computers improve students' performances. The examples of successes are isolated cases.

3. The current use of computers is uninspired and cannot facilitate the learning process. Teachers lack the time needed to develop good applications. Most of the educational software is flawed. Moreover, they cannot be expected to meet the needs of all students or teachers.

4. The training of the future workforce is not an excuse since most employers have to train employees for specific job assignment.
5. The money diverted to computers stifles other programs such as music, arts, and physical education, which are essential for the rounded development of the student.
6. Even if the Internet improves learning, no one is yet to prove that the advantages of teaching using the Internet significantly outweigh the advantages of using other cheaper information media.
7. Every new technology brings with it positive and

negative impact. Nobody has taken time to analyze the negative impact of exposing children to the Internet may have on their social development.

11.3   Sitting On the Fence?

On which side of the coin are you? The mere fact that you are reading this book suggests that you are interested in this issue. I personally believe that if properly used, technology can make a positive difference in the classroom. I do not consider those who criticize the way technology is used in the classroom as enemies. In fact, they are the best friends of technology in the classroom. It would be by genuinely addressing some of the concerns of the doubters that the supporters can optimize the benefits of technology in education.

11.4   Resources and References

Listed below are references to sites that you may use to increase your understanding of the issues involved in teaching using the Internet. As the Internet continues to evolve, some of the sites listed in these references may change as well. If this is the case, use a search engine to find the resources you need.

1. **The Computer Delusion**
   http://www.theatlantic.com/issues/97jul/computer.html
   Todd Oppenheimer argues that there is no good evidence that most uses of computers significantly improve teaching and learning, despite all the money spent on computers.

2. **High-Tech Schools and Low-Tech Teaching**
   http://www.edweek.org/ew/vol-16/34cuban.h16
   Larry Cuban believes that many students are not learning in the so-called technology schools.

3. **Training Enhances computer Usage**
   http://www.edweek.org/ew/vol-16/29jost.h16
   The findings of a poll result indicate that superintendents and teachers agree that computers could be used more effectively if teachers received adequate training.

4. **Training Firm to Attract Teachers**
   http://www.edweek.org/ew/vol-15/22comput.h15
   A private training firm wants to train teachers to use technology properly in the classroom.

6. **Business Group for Technology Training**
   http://www.edweek.org/ew/vol-18/25tech.h18
   A Business Group calls for More Technology Training
   for teachers so that they can produce computer literate
   students.

7. **Technology Brings Benefits and Dangers**
   http://www.edweek.org/ew/vol-17/38sherm.h17
   The dangers of using the Internet in the classroom
   are highlighted by Thomas Sherman, Education
   Week, June 3, 1998.

8. **Internet and Technology**
   http://www.edweek.org/context/politics/internet.htm:
   This site gives an overview of the Clinton's
   Administration agenda on Education. Moreover,
   there is the Education Week's Archives on technology
   and education related issues.

9. **Education Headlines**
   http://www.ed.gov
   The president's policy on technological education are
   highlighted at this site.

10. **Report on Technology and Education**
    http://www.ed.gov/Technology/Plan/NatTechPlan/
    A Report to the Nation on Technology and Education
    by the Department of education, June 29, 1996.

11. **Education Statistics**
    http://nces.ed.gov/pubs/97944.html
    A survey on the use of advanced telecommunications
    in U.S. Public Elementary and Secondary Schools is
    provided at this site.

12. **Pedagogy Publications**
    http://www.ilt.columbia.edu/Publications/index.html
    This sites provides useful reading information for teachers who are interested in pedagogical issues regarding the reform of our public schools.

13 **Technology to Support Education Reform**
    http://www.ed.gov/pubs/EdReformStudies/
    TechReforms/
    This site discusses issues such as how technology affects student learning, why reforms fail, and implementation issues. There are also excellent references on the site.

14. **Quality Education Data**
    http://www.infomall.org:80/Showcase/QED/
    The site provides data on education trend in US public schools.

15. **Fostering the Use of Educational Technology**
    http://www.rand.org/publications/MR/MR682/
    contents.html
    This site contains information on the current use and effectiveness of educational technologies.

16. **Using Technology in Education**
    http://www.algonquinc.on.ca/edtech/
    index.html#main1
    Apart from learning about educational technologies, the site gives information on learning to use technology, changes in education due to technology, and on using multimedia in the classroom.

17. **The New Media and Learning**
    http://www.prospect.org/archives/27/27star.html
    An interesting article on the media and learning is available at this site.

18. **Technology News**
    http://theatlantic.com/tech/tech.htm
    If you like education and technology news, this is one of the sites to browse.

19. **Tech-Learning**
    http://www.techlearning.com
    This site provides educators with ideas, tools, and resources for integrating technology into K-12 schools, classrooms, and curriculum.

20. **Virtual Reality on the Web Using Quick Time VR:**
    http://www.wnet.org/wnetschool/primer/qtvr.html:
    This site should give the reader an idea of projects suitable for use on the Internet.

21. **The Thornburg Center**
    http://www.tcpd.org
    The Thornburg Center is a world-renowned consulting firm that focuses on the impact of emerging technologies on Education, among others. It is a good source for education news and for getting speakers.

22. **The Condition of Education 1998, Indicator 4**
    http://nces.ed.gov/pubs98/condition98/
    c9804a01.html
    This site provides statistics on Internet access in public and private schools in the United States.

23. Learning in the Real World

http://www.realworld.org

Learning in the Real World is a nonprofit organization that looks at issues involved in implementing education technologies. The organization makes research grants to university investigators to develop, analyze and distribute information on how education technology affects the development of children.

Part V

Appendices: Acceptable Use Policies (AUPs)

Many school systems and colleges provide free Internet access and other network services to their employees. In return, employees (or other users of these services) are expected to behave in an honest and responsible way while using these services. Acceptable Use Policies give a set of guidelines that govern the use of a particular provider's Internet service or other networks. Below are two examples of AUPs. We hope these will provide some guiding principles as you design an AUP that is suitable to your particular environment.

Appendix A: Hamilton County AUP[1]

Revised 2002
Telecommunications Employee
Acceptable Use Policy
For Internet & Electronic Mail Access

The Internet and email provide invaluable resources and communications to Hamilton County employees. Employees accessing the Internet are representing the Hamilton County School System and therefore have a responsibility to use the Internet in a productive manner

[1] Reproduced with permission of the Hamilton County School System

that meets the ethical standards of an educational institution.

Our goal is to provide Internet and e-mail access to facilitate resource sharing, innovation, and communication as a tool to promote educational excellence. As a condition of using Hamilton County Department of Education's telecommunications equipment, I understand that access to telecommunication networks (e.g., e-mail, the internet) is a privilege, and agree to the following:

ACCEPTABLE USE

1. The use of the Internet must be in support of education and research, and be consistent with educational standards and objectives of Hamilton County Schools.
2. Transmission or storage of any material in violation of any U.S. or state regulation is prohibited. Any material that is copyrighted, threatening, offensive, obscene, or otherwise intended to harass or demean recipients, must not be transmitted.
3. E-mail communications should be used for professional reasons and utilized in an ethical and lawful manner. There is **no expectation of privacy** when communicating over the network via the Internet or e-mail. Accessing personal e-mail accounts are prohibited on the HCDE network; i.e., CompuServe and AOL.
4. Private, commercial or illegal use is prohibited. This prohibition extends to the use of the Internet or other electronic media equipment to access, store, or display pornographic or other offensive material.
5. Programs that infiltrate computing systems and/or damage software components are prohibited.

6. Files, data, or information of others must not be improperly accessed or misused.
7. User accounts must not be shared or left open and unattended.
8. Backup copies and transfer of data between computers of documents and files are the responsibility of the user.
9. Anonymous communications are not allowed.
10. Security violations must be reported to the Principal/ Department Director immediately.
11. Personal information must be given out only in an instructional context or in the performance of the Hamilton County Schools' business.
12. Remote access to the HCDEs' network is not allowed unless approved in writing by the Director of Information Services.
13. Any downloaded material must be in support of education and research and be consistent with educational standards and objectives of Hamilton County Schools. To prevent viruses to the HCDE equipment, prior to downloading, ensure the antivirus software has been updated with the latest files. Download only software that you have a legal right to download. If a download is going to require excessive bandwidth of the network, obtain permission from the Principal/Departmental Director before proceeding with the download.
14. Messages must be deleted regularly to conserve space. File or delete your sent items folder and empty the deleted items folder on a weekly basis. If you receive large files, delete them from email after you have saved and confirmed that the files have been saved.

15. Malicious attempts to harm or destroy hardware, software, or data are prohibited.
16. Any action that violates existing Board policy or public law is prohibited.
17. Refer to the Website Design Guidelines and Policies document that resides on the HCDE Intranet website regarding school based website creations at **http:// home.hcde.org**.

Hamilton County Department of Education has taken reasonable measures to prevent obscene and controversial materials from appearing on our network, but cannot completely control access to all inappropriate materials. Hamilton County Department of Education firmly believes that the valuable information, interaction and communication available on this worldwide network far outweighs the possibility that users may procure material that is not consistent with the educational goals of the school system.

I have read and agree to comply with the Hamilton County Department of Education Acceptable Use Policy. I understand that any violations of these regulations are unethical, potentially illegal, and may constitute a criminal offense. Should I commit any violation, my access privileges may be revoked and disciplinary action may be taken, up to and including termination of employment.

As a Hamilton County Department of Education employee, your acceptance is implied by your use of Hamilton County Department of Education equipment.

Employee's Name (Please Print)　　　Location

Employee's Signature　　　Date

Student Access Release and Authorization Form

As a user of the Hamilton County School System computer network and the Internet, I hereby agree to comply with the Hamilton County Department of Education AUP agreement while under the jurisdiction of the Hamilton County School System. Should I commit any violation, my access privileges may be revoked and disciplinary action may be taken, up to and including suspension/ expulsion. Deliberate misuse resulting in hardware and / or software damage will be the financial responsibility of the parent/guardian.

Student Signature:_____Date:_____

As the parent or legal guardian of the student signing above, I grant permission for him/her to access networked computer services, such as electronic mail (e-mail) and the Internet. I understand that he/she is expected to use good judgment and to follow the rules and guidelines in making contact on the telecommunication network (e.g. e-mail, the Internet). The Hamilton County Department of Education cannot be responsible for ideas and concepts that he/she may gain by his/her use of the Internet. I further understand that deliberate misuse by the student resulting in hardware and/or software damage will be the responsibility of the parent/guardian.

I understand and accept the conditions stated above and agree to hold harmless and release from liability the school and Hamilton County Department of Education.

Parent/guardian signature:_____

Date:_____

Student name:_____

School:_____Grade:_____

Student SSN: _____

Birth date: _____

Home Address and Zip Code:

_____

Home Phone:_____

Work Phone (if applicable)_____

Appendix B: University of Tennessee at Chattanooga AUP[2]

While the Information Technology Division (ITD) has the primary responsibility for the creation and implementation of a cost-effective information infrastructure in which authorized users (e.g., students, faculty, staff, alumni, consultants, authorized affiliates, outside clients) can create and share intellectual and administrative information, the principles described in this AUP document apply to all UTC computing and networking facilities that are provided for use by the users for legitimate purposes relating to education, research, administration, and outreach activities of the University. These principles do not apply to open access to library materials available to the general public, which are addressed in the UTC Libraries' "Internet Access Policy."

The term, "UTC Technology Resources," as addressed in this document is defined but not limited to include any computers, computer systems, software applications, networks (including telecommunications equipment, e.g., routers, switches), or other devices that are owned by UTC. All devices connected to the UTC network that are not owned by UTC are expected to follow the principles in this AUP. UTC Technology Resources include all electronic information, institutional data, documents, messages (including email), programs or system software, or configuration files that are stored, executed, or transmitted via University computers, networks, or other information systems.

[2] Reproduced with permission of the University of Tennessee at Chattanooga

The responsibilities and obligations according to these Acceptable Use Practices include:

Purpose

The purpose of this document, UTC Acceptable Use Practices (AUP), is to implement UT's Use of Information Technology Resources (Section 175, Part 01, of UT's Fiscal Policy Manual). The community at UTC is based on principles of honesty, academic integrity, respect for others, and respect for others' privacy and property. UTC seeks to:

- Protect the confidentiality of data and the privacy of its users, to the extent allowed under State and federal law, including the Tennessee Public Records Act;
- Safeguard the integrity of UTC data and IT resources and maintain the reasonable availability of UTC IT resources;
- Preserve UTC policies regarding harassment and the safety of individuals;
- Minimize University liability from community use of IT resources;
- Appropriately respond to the misuse of University IT resources;
- Appropriately respond to claims of infringement of electronically posted copies of copyrighted materials; and
- Ensure that the use of electronic communications complies with the provisions of the Practices.

Responsibilities

Each departmental unit is responsible for the security of their systems and networks and may apply more stringent security policies than those detailed herein while connected to UTC Technology Resources; however, they must follow these principles as a minimum or risk losing connectivity to UTC networks.

ITD is responsible for identifying a campus Information Security Officer who will coordinate and facilitate the campus Information Security Program with collaboration from the UTC Computer Security Committee. This program will include but not be limited to the following:

1. Development and implementation of information security policies, standards, controls, procedures, and practices as defined in UT Fiscal Policy Section 175, Part 01; Use of Information Technology Resources in order to protect UTC IT resources.

2. Development of a security awareness and training program for users, system administrators, and designated security officers.

3. Establishment of a central repository for recording, tracking, and resolving security related incidents through collaboration with responsible organizations.

4. Recommendations for cost-effective security solutions for unit/departmental systems, network administrators, and designated security officers.

5. Establishment of UTC's Best Practices Guidelines for Information Technology Resource Use to include but not limited to:

- User accountability requirements, e.g., user identification and authentication, account administration, and password integrity;
- Public access restrictions and limitations;
- Authorized access;
- System and data integrity;
- Auditing;
- File backup and recovery;
- Disaster recovery;
- Malicious code protection;
- Configuration security;
- Guest account guidelines;
- Unattended equipment; and
- Incident reporting, response and escalation procedures.

System & LAN Administrator Responsibilities

System and LAN administrator privileges on UTC IT resources confer substantial authority as well as responsibility to all other connected systems and networks. When an incident is reported or discovered, the system administrator will be contacted in order to resolve the situation.

In an emergency situation, the UTC Information Security Officer may direct that systems, in which intrusions are detected or that are not properly maintained for security vulnerabilities, be disconnected from all other UTC IT resources to isolate the intrusion and to protect other systems connected to the network until assurance can be made that the problem has been adequately resolved and will not reoccur.

System and LAN administrators are responsible for the implementation of appropriate technical security on their computer systems. They must make every effort to remain familiar with the changing security technology that relates to their system and continually analyze technical vulnerabilities and their resulting security implications. All systems must be maintained with critical and security related vendor supplied patches at all times. Stored authentication data (e.g., password files, encryption keys, certificates, personal identification numbers, and access codes) must be appropriately protected with access controls, encryption, shadowing, etc.

Systems and LAN administrators or designated security officers may supplement this document with unit specific and/or more stringent guidelines for their users but cannot lessen these principles. System and LAN administrators and designated security officers are encouraged to become trained and certified through the ITD; however, equivalent prior training and experience may be sufficient.

System and LAN administrators shall perform their duties fairly, in cooperation with the user community, the University administration, and in accordance with University policies. System and LAN administrators shall respect the privacy of users unless investigating reports of abuse of privileges and shall refer all substantiated violations to the appropriate authority (e.g., Student Honor Court, Personnel Services) for disciplinary action.

System and LAN administrators are responsible for ensuring appropriate security is enabled and enforced in order to protect the UTC network to which it is connected.

Systems and LANs that are not properly maintained for security vulnerabilities may, after repeated warnings, be disconnected by ITD from all other UTC IT resources to protect other systems connected to the network until assurance can be made that the problems have been adequately resolved and will not reoccur.

User Responsibilities

While the University recognizes the role of privacy in an institution of higher learning and every attempt will be made to honor that ideal, there should be no expectation of privacy of information stored on or sent through University owned information systems and communications infrastructure (except for research and certain other protected records that have been declared confidential by the President of the University and approved by the State Attorney General).

All users are expected to act in a responsible, ethical, and legal manner with the understanding that UTC Technology Resources are conducted in a public forum. Users must respect the rights of others (especially rights of privacy and confidentiality); freedom of expression; intellectual property rights; State and federal laws, including the Family Educational Rights and Privacy Act (FERPA); and due process.

Users are required to follow the established guidelines and procedures described in these principles. Although system administrators or designated security officers strive to provide and preserve the security and integrity of files, account numbers, authorization codes, and passwords; security can be breached through actions or causes beyond their reasonable control. Therefore, users are urged to safeguard their data, personal information, passwords, and authorization codes by taking full advantage of file security mechanisms built into the computer's operating system.

Users granted administrative or operator privileges (e.g., root or Administrator) to systems are also responsible for following the principles for system administrators delineated above.

User accountability is established through the assignment of a unique user account name (ID) and protected with some form of authentication (e.g., a password). Users are REQUIRED to protect their individual account and not share it with others for their use, nor utilize another user's account for any reason. Since passwords are typically the first line of defense to UTC Technology Resources, users should choose passwords carefully and comply with UTC password guidelines for effective password protection. Users are responsible for any electronic messages that are transmitted from their accounts.

Compliance

The University does not routinely examine the content of a user's account space and any storage devices of University owned equipment; however, it reserves the right to investigate the use of that account and storage and inspect the contents when deemed necessary.

The University reserves the right to establish procedures designed to protect authorized users from the effects of abuse or negligence by limiting, restricting, or terminating use of UTC Technology Resources; or by inspecting, copying, removing, or altering any data, file, or system resource which might be reasonably construed as undermining authorized use.

System administrators or designated security officers will ensure that user authentication is required before access to any restricted UTC Technology Resources is granted. All users of UTC Technology Resources agree to the following rules and responsibilities:

- No one shall knowingly or willingly interfere with the security mechanisms or integrity of UTC Technology Resources. Users shall not attempt to circumvent data protection schemes or exploit security loopholes.

- No one shall knowingly create, install, execute, or distribute any malicious code (e.g., virus, Trojan Horse, worm) or another surreptitiously destructive program on any UTC Technology Resource, except for as explicitly authorized by the campus Information Security Officer and only for the express purpose of improving campus security practices and after special precautions are taken.

- No one shall interfere with the intended use of UTC Technology Resources. All users shall share computing resources (e.g., bandwidth) in an ethical and fair manner and not unduly interfere with use by other authorized users.

- No one shall use UTC Technology Resources to attempt unauthorized use, or interfere with the legitimate use by authorized users, of other computers or networks elsewhere users are responsible for adhering to the policies and principles of such networks. UTC cannot and will not extend any protection to users who violate external network policies. Abuse of networks or computers at other sites through the use of UTC Technology Resources will be treated as an abuse of UTC Technology Resource privileges.

• No one shall use UTC Technology Resources for individual financial or commercial gain; use of these resources, except for authorized University business, is prohibited.

• No one shall perform, participate, encourage, or conceal any unauthorized use or attempts of unauthorized use of UTC Technology Resources.

• No one shall use a system either directly attached to UTC Technology Resources or through wireless means to capture data packets (e.g., "sniffer") except for authorized or other official University business.

• No one shall use UTC Technology Resources to transmit abusive, threatening, or harassing material, chain letters, spam, or communications prohibited by state or federal laws.

• No one shall launch, intentionally or otherwise, denial of service attacks against other users, systems, or networks.

• No one shall abuse the policies of any newsgroups, mailing lists, and other public forums through which they participate from a University account.

• No one shall connect any computer or network system to any UTC network (e.g., direct connection, direct dial-in access, or wireless access) without following the Security Best Practices guidelines, which, at a minimum, requires user identification and authentication.

- No one shall misrepresent his or her identity or relationship to the University for the purpose of accessing or attempting unauthorized access to UTC Technology Resources nor misrepresent his or her identity to other networks (e.g., IP address or email address "spoofing") from UTC Technology Resources.

- No user shall access (e.g., read, write, modify, delete, copy, move) another user's files or electronic mail without the owner's permission except by system and LAN administrators duly authorized by the official policies and procedures applicable. In addition, It is the individual user's responsibility to protect his/her files.

- No one shall use UTC Technology Resources in violation of applicable patent protection and authorizations, copyrights, license agreements, other contracts, State or federal laws, or by University rules or regulations.

- No one shall place confidential information on computers without appropriately protecting it as outlined in the UTC Security Best Practice Guidelines. The University cannot guarantee the privacy of files, electronic mail, or other information stored or transmitted on UTC Technology Resources.

- No one shall compromise the privacy of others or the confidentiality of the information contained on UTC Technology Resources.

Violations

Abuse of UTC policies or standards, abuse of UTC Technology Resources, or abuse of other sites through the use of UTC Technology Resources may result in termination of access, disciplinary review, expulsion, termination of employment, legal action, and/or other appropriate disciplinary action.

Notification will be made to the appropriate UTC office, e.g., Personnel Services, Academic Personnel, Student Honor Court, Dean of Student Development, General Counsel, UTC police, or local, State and federal law enforcement agencies.

System administrators and designated security officers will, when necessary, work with other University offices such as the UTC Dean of Students, UTC Police, schools' and colleges' disciplinary councils, the General Counsel, Personnel Services, Academic Personnel, and others in the resolution of security incidents.

The University Security Officer shall establish procedures for isolating and/or disconnecting systems from the network while assessing any suspected or reported security incident in order to minimize risk to the rest of the UTC network. In the event of a legal investigation, the University reserves the right to isolate the system and "lock it down" to preserve evidence during investigation by law enforcement agencies.

Reporting Security Incidents & Infractions

Users are expected to report any information concerning instances in which they suspect or have evidence that the above principles have been or are being violated.

Reports about suspected violations of these principles should be directed to buse@utc.edu for customer relations regarding inappropriate public behavior or for network operations or infrastructure. Receipt of incident reports will be acknowledged and investigated in a timely manner. When a complaint of possible system or account misuse is reported to the University, the validity of the incident will be investigated per standard operating procedures. Any incidents that appear to be valid are forwarded to the appropriate UTC office with all supporting documentation or evidence gathered for investigation and resolution. All parties will be informed of the resolution of such incidents.

Related Documents

- Digital Millennium Copyright Act (DMCA) (http://www.educause.edu/issues/dmca.html)
- Ethical Use Policy, University of Tennessee at Chattanooga Lupton Library (http://www.lib.utc.edu/code.html)
- Disciplinary Actions, UT Personnel Procedure, Section 500, Proc. 525 (http://admin.tennessee.edu/hr/policies/525pol.html)
- Use of Information Technology Resources, Section 135, Part 01 of University of Tennessee Fiscal Policy (http://admin.tennessee.edu/acs/5135-01.htm)
- Software Copyright Compliance and License Agreements, Section 135, Part 02 of University Fiscal Policy (http://admin.tennessee.edu/acs/5135-02.htm)
- University of Tennessee Work Rules, Rule 9 of the Personnel Policy Section 500, Policy 580 (http://admin.tennessee.edu/hr/policies/580pol.html)

- State of Tennessee Internet Acceptable Use Policy
  (http://www.state.tn.us/finance/oir/policy/aup/int-aup.htm)
- State of Tennessee Information Technology Policies
  (http://www.state.tn.us/finance/oir/policy/index.htm)
- State of Tennessee E-mail Acceptable Use Policy
  (http://www.state.tn.us/finance/oir/policy/aup/aupemail2.html)

UTC Code of Computing Practice

The UTC Information Technology Division has the responsibility for securing its computing system to a reasonable and economically feasible degree against unauthorized access, while making the system accessible for legitimate and innovative uses. This responsibility includes informing persons who use the computer system of expected standards of conduct and encouraging their application. It is important for you to practice ethical behavior in computing activities because you have access to many valuable and sensitive resources and your computing practices can adversely affect the work of other people.

Although most people act responsibly, the few who do not, either through ignorance or by intent, have the potential for disrupting everyone's work.

The list below constitutes a code of computing practice for all persons using the UTC system. Disciplinary action for violating the code shall be governed by the applicable provisions of student handbooks, faculty and staff handbooks, personnel policy manuals for The University of Tennessee, and the Computer Crimes Act of The State of Tennessee.

- You are responsible for being aware of and following the published procedures for accessing the UTC computing system.
- You must use only the computer accounts that have been authorized for your use. You are required to identify all of your computing work with your name and assigned account codes so that responsibility for the work can be determined and you can be contacted in unusual situations, e.g., the return of misplaced output.
- You are responsible for the use of your computer accounts. You should make appropriate use of system-provided protection features such as passwords, and you should take precautions against others obtaining access to your computer resources. Do not make your account available to others for any purpose. If you require assistance in using your accounts, you should contact UTC Help Desk 755-4000.
- You must use your computer accounts only for the purpose for which they are authorized. For example, unsponsored research codes must not be used for sponsored research work or private consulting.
- Do not access or copy the programs, files or data belonging to other persons or to UTC without prior authorization to do so. Do not attempt to access files for which you do not have authorization. Programs, subroutines and data provided by UTC are not to be taken to other computer sites without permission. You may use software on UTC computers only if it has been legally obtained and

its use does not violate any license or copyright restriction. Do not use programs at UTC that were obtained from other computer sites unless they are in the public domain or authorization to use them at UTC has been obtained.

- To minimize the impact of your work on the work of other persons, you must not attempt to encroach on others' use of the facilities or deprive them of resources.
- Do not attempt to modify system facilities.
- Do not attempt to subvert the restrictions associated with your computer accounts.

The code is intended to work to the benefit of all who use the UTC system by encouraging responsible use of scarce computer resources. So that UTC ITD can better serve you, feedback on the code is welcome.

Notes

Notes

Notes

Notes

About the Author

Dr. Aniekan Ebiefung is a University of Chattanooga Foundation Professor of Mathematics at the University of Tennessee at Chatanooga. Professor Ebiefung holds Bachelor of Science degrees in Mathematics and Statistics (with First Class Honors) from the University of Calabar, Master of Science in Mathematics from Howard University, and Ph.D in Mathematical Sciences from Clemson University. He has held faculty positions at Calabar Polytechnic; University of Cross River State; Federal University of Technology, Owerri; Howard University; Clemson University; and the University of Tennessee at Chattanooga.

Dr. Ebiefung has received many research grants and teaching awards, including the 1993 Oakridge Associated Universities Junior Faculty Enhancement Award in Mathematics and Computer Science, Student Government Association Outstanding Professor Award 1993-4, the 1998 Southeastern Inform Best Paper Award in Quantitative Theory and Methods Track, and the University of Chattanooga Foundation Professorship.

Professor Ebiefung has received over 30 grants and has organized, both locally and internationally, workshops, seminars and discussion groups on problem solving and on the use of the Internet in teaching. He has consulted for the National Science Foundation, the Tennessee Higher Education Commission, and the Educational Testing Service through various grant activities. He is listed in *Who's Who in American Education* and *Who's Who in the World*, among others.

Dr. Ebiefung and his wife, Anne, have three children: Ediobong, Uduak, and Mary Ann.